LAW SCHOOL FLOWCHARTS

Also from Kaplan PMBR:

Kaplan PMBR FINALS: Civil Procedure

Kaplan PMBR FINALS: Conflicts of Law

Kaplan PMBR FINALS: Constitutional Law

Kaplan PMBR FINALS: Contracts

Kaplan PMBR FINALS: Corporations

Kaplan PMBR FINALS: Criminal Law

Kaplan PMBR FINALS: Criminal Procedure

Kaplan PMBR FINALS: Evidence

Kaplan PMBR FINALS: Family Law

Kaplan PMBR FINALS: Property

Kaplan PMBR FINALS: Remedies

Kaplan PMBR FINALS: Torts

Kaplan PMBR FINALS: Trusts

Kaplan PMBR FINALS: Wills

Kaplan PMBR: MBE Flashcards

Kaplan PMBR: MPRE

Kaplan PMBR: MPT

LAW SCHOOL FLOWCHARTS

Nicole Lefton, Esq.
Curriculum Director
Kaplan PMBR

© 2009 by Kaplan, Inc.

Published by Kaplan Publishing, a division of Kaplan, Inc.
1 Liberty Plaza, 24th Floor
New York, NY 10006

Printed in the United States of America

10 9 8 7 6 5 4 3 2 1

ISBN-13: 978-1-60714-329-1

Kaplan Publishing books are available at special quantity discounts to use for sales promotions, employee premiums, or educational purposes. Please email our Special Sales Department to order or for more information at kaplanpublishing@kaplan.com, or write to Kaplan Publishing, 1 Liberty Plaza, 24th Floor, New York, NY 10006.

Presenting Kaplan PMBR.
Focused on your success.

Dear First Year law Student,

Your legal career is on the horizon. Succeeding in law school is the first step to getting there. Kaplan PMBR provides a range of products and services to help you stay ahead in classes, on midterms and finals, and when it's time to study for the Bar exam.

Start law school with an authoritative guide through legal subjects: *Law School Flowcharts* from Kaplan PMBR.
A collection of detailed flowcharts designed to give you an overview of core 1L subjects. You can use them throughout law school, when you prep for the Bar, and when you're a practicing attorney.

Our exclusive *FINALS* series gives you more advantages.
They're comprehensive outlines of 1L and 2L subjects, and valuable practice questions with detailed answers and explanations. Titles in the series include: Torts, Property, Contracts, Evidence, and more. Get them all, and get the best advantage.

Go to KaplanPMBR.com for support now and in the future.
You'll find information and resources, plus our online bookstore offering our *FINALS* series, plus study guides, innovative outlines, versatile online resources, and more.

That's just the start. Call 1-800-523-0777, or go to KaplanPMBR.com to learn all the ways we can help you today, and tomorrow.

Sincerely,

Kaplan PMBR

1. JURISDICTION

PERSONAL JURISDICTION

In Personam: Jurisdiction over Δ personally and/or his property

In Rem: Jurisdiction over a ***particular item*** of Δ's property. Ct has power to adjudicate rights of ***all persons*** in world over the property.

Quasi-in-Rem: Ct has jurisdiction over ***particular individuals*** with respect to specific property.

Types
- In personam.
- In-Rem.
- Quasi-In-Rem does ***not*** bind Δ personally.

Jurisdiction based upon
- Personal service inside forum state.
- Domiciliary.
- Consent.
- Minimum contacts.
- Long-Arm statutes within 100 miles of Federal Ct.

SUBJECT MATTER JURISDICTION (Federal question jurisdiction)

Extends → To all civil actions arising under U.S. Constitution, treaties and federal laws.

Amount in controversy → No minimum amount required.

Diversity → No diversity of parties required.

Joinder of claims → If subject matter jurisdiction exists, federal court may add (append) related state law actions to federal claim.

DIVERSITY JURISDICTION

Requirements
- Diversity Δ & π = different states
- $75,000 + amount in controversy
- Aggregation of amount allowed

Erie doctrine (Fed. Ct.)
- Must apply substantive law of forum st.
- Procedural rules apply fed. rules of civil procedure.

Pendent or Supplemental Jurisdiction
- π has both a fed & state claim against Δ.
- Fed. Ct. may join both claims

2. VENUE

VENUE
(Judicial district where action may be brought)

Diversity cases
- District where any Δ resides.
- Where claim occurred.
- Or substantial part of claim occurred.

Federal claim cases
- (i) Where any Δ resides.
- (ii) Where property that is subject of action is located.
- If (i) & (ii) cannot be satisfied then wherever Δ can be found.

Corporate Residency
- Corporate Δ resides where it has sufficient contacts.
- Corporate π resides in state of its incorporation.

TRANSFER OF VENUE
(Fed. Ct. may transfer venue to another district)

Factors
- Convenience of parties.
- Convenience of witnesses.
- Forum non conveniens
- Where material event occurred.

Law applicable upon transfer
- Law of transferor Ct. generally applies
- Transferee Ct. law applies if original venue was improper.

REMOVAL JURISDICTION

Permitted
- Δ may remove a fed. question action from state to fed. ct.

Limitation
- Diversity removal **not** permitted if one of Δs is a citizen of the same state as the π.

Dismissal of nondiverse party.

Removal ⟶ Allowable

If diversity does not exist because a party is a co-citizen of an opposing party their removal is permitted if non-diverse parties are thereafter dismissed.

KAPLAN pmbr

3. PRETRIAL MOTION PRACTICE

MOTION TO DISMISS (Fed. Rule 12b)

Grounds for dismissal
- Lack of sub. matter jurisdiction.
- Lack of personal jurisdiction.
- Improper venue.
- Insufficient process.
- Failure to state a claim.
- Failure to join necessary party.

Judgment on pleadings (Fed. Rule 12c)
- After all pleadings completed.
- Motion denied unless there are no facts to support cause of action.

Summary Judgment
- Motion may be made at any time usually after pleadings.
- Motion granted if no genuine issue of material fact exists.

COLLATERAL ATTACK

Personal Jurisdiction

Δ never makes an appearance & default judgment is entered.

Can Δ collaterally attack for lack of personal jurisdiction? Yes, but if Δ loses on personal jurisdiction issue, default judgment stands.

Summary Judgment
- Can Δ collaterally attack judg. bec. of lack of subj. matter jurisdiction?
- Yes, if judgment was by default. No, if it was a contested action.

CONSOLIDATION

Fed. Rule 12(g)
- Requires consolidation of defenses into motion.
- Failure to consolidate leads to waiver.

WAIVER
- Defenses waived if not pleaded.
  - Lack of personal jurisdiction.
  - Improper venue.
  - Insufficient of process.

NO WAIVER
- Defenses preserved if not originally pleaded.
  - Failure to state a claim.
  - Failure to join necessary party.

4. JOINDER

JOINDER OF CLAIMS

Permitted (Permissive) → Party allowed to join as many claims as she has against opposing party.

Compelled (Compulsory)
- If failure to join could result in splitting of cause of action.
- Example: π has suffered both property loss & personal injury resulting from auto accident.

JOINDER OF PARTIES

Permissive
- Multiple πs may join if each seeks relief on same claim from same transaction.
- One π may join several Δs in one claim that arises from same transaction.

NECESSARY (INDISPENSABLE PARTIES)

Motion to Dismiss
- May be granted for failure to join indispensible party.
- Exception: If joinder is impossible (e.g. joinder would destroy diversity) action may proceed w/ outsider viewed as a necessary *not* indispensable party.

IMPLEADER

3rd party practice to add persons to the suit
- If person "is or may be liable" to Δ.
- Δ seeks indemnity or contribution.

INTERPLEADER

Person has interest in property that is subject of litigation.
- "Stakeholder" may bring in other claimants to decide matter in a single law suit.
- In personam action and court must have personal jurisdiction over all parties.

KAPLAN pmbr

5. BINDING EFFECT OF JUDGMENT

RES JUDICATA
(Applies in civil actions *NOT* criminal cases.)

Claim Preclusion

Precludes re-litigation of claim if final judgment is rendered.

Example: p sues Δ for negligence. Judgment rendered for Δ. p cannot sue again for same cause of action.

Parties Bound

Same parties are bound.

Non-parties not bound.

SPLITTING A CLAIM

Merger

p wins an earlier lawsuit, his cause of action *merges* w/the judgment and he cannot sue again.

Bar

If Δ wins, the p is "barred" by the adverse judgment and cannot sue again.

COLLATERAL ESTOPPEL
(Applies in both civil and criminal cases.)

Issue Preclusion (Civil case)

A judgment for p or Δ precludes relitigation of same issues by same parties.

Example: p sues Δ for negligence. p is found to be contributorily negligent. The issue of contributory negligence cannot be relitigated.

Criminal Case

Δ asserts intoxication as defense in a larceny prosecution. Jury finds Δ was not intoxicated when he stole prop. Δ now prosecuted for battery (arising out of same incident) because he struck victim when he took her prop. He cannot assert intoxication as a defense to battery.

NON-MUTUAL COLLATERAL ESTOPPEL

Cannot be used against a non-party to the previous action.

Can a non-party use collateral estoppel against someone who was a party?

Yes, as a "defensive shield" (e.g., A is involved in an auto accident w/B, a driver for C Corp. A sues B for negligence and losses. A cannot sue C).

Yes, as an "offensive sword" (e.g. SEC sued Δ for stock fraud and won. A, private p, sued Δ for same violation established in SEC action, p can establish violation on Δ's part based on SEC action.

6. DISCOVERY

DISCOVERY DEVICES
- Oral deposition
- Written deposition
- Interrogatories
- Document production
- Physical/mental exam

INFORMATION REQUESTED
- Must be relevant.
- Privileged matter not discoverable.
- Insurance agreements discoverable.
- Qualified immunity: Attorney's work product.
- Limited discovery: Expert trial witnesses.

PROCEDURAL ASPECTS OF DISCOVERY
- Motion to compel where there has been a failure to comply w/discovery request.
- Protective order: Ct. may grant a protective order over confidential documents.

DISCOVERY SANCTIONS
- Discovery conference (failure to participate may result in sanctions).
- Discovery request (failure to supply info may result in sanctions).
- Discovery motions and discovery requests must be signed by attorney. If info is false, attorney may also be sanctioned.

1. FEDERAL JUDICIAL AUTHORITY

ARTICLE III — vests the judicial power in the Supreme Court and such inferior courts as Congress may establish; jurisdiction limited to "cases and controversies." Compare: Article I Courts (tax courts, courts in the District of Columbia) are vested with administrative, as well as judicial functions; no lifetime tenure for Article I judges. Role of Congress: plenary power both to establish lower federal courts and to confer and remove jurisdiction over Article III courts.
Note that Article III courts may not give advisory opinions, although state courts may do so

Organization of the Federal Court System

POWER OF JUDICIAL REVIEW — _Marbury v Madison_ — held that the Supreme Court may determine the constitutionality of acts of other branches of government; federal courts may also review state court decisions

JURISDICTION OF THE SUPREME COURT — Original (trial level) — extends to "all cases affecting Ambassadors, other public Ministers and Consuls, and those in which a State shall be a Party"; Congress may neither enlarge nor restrict, but may give concurrent jurisdiction to lower federal courts (except in cases between 2 or more states where the Supreme Court has exclusive jurisdiction) Appellate— extends to all other Article III cases and controversies; Congress may broadly regulate, but may not preclude review of an entire class of cases

TWO STATUTORY MEANS — Provided by Congress to invoke the Supreme Court's Appellate Jurisdiction: 1. Appeal (mandatory review)— applies to decisions of 3-judge federal district courts
2. Certiorari (discretionary; 4 or more justices vote to hear a case) — applies to decisions of US Courts of Appeal state courts regarding federal law issues, and decisions of the highest

(continued)

1. FEDERAL JUDICIAL AUTHORITY *(continued)*

Judicial Review (doctrine empowering federal courts to refuse to hear a case, despite subject matter jurisdiction)

STANDING — concrete personal stake in the outcome is required by Article III — Injury in Fact — specific, not theoretical, injury must arise from the government conduct being complained of; usually economic injury, but need not be — Redressibility (Causation) — the relief sought must eliminate the harm alleged; plaintiff's injury must be within the "zone of interests" Congress meant to protect — Prudential Limitations — self-imposed by the Court; no "citizen" standing for abstract, generalized grievances; a corporation has standing to challenge a federal statute where the injury is to the organization itself; no third party standing, unless plaintiff herself has suffered injury which adversely affects her relationship with third parties, who have difficulty asserting their own rights; no taxpayer standing because the interest is too remote, except a federal taxpayer has standing to make an establishment clause challenge to an expenditure which exceeds some specific limitation on the taxing and spending power *(Flast v Cohen)*

MOOTNESS — a case brought too late; an actual controversy must exist at all stages of review, unless the issue is capable of repetition, yet evading review (pregnancy, elections)

RIPENESS — a case brought too early; a genuine, immediate threat of harm must exist (no declaratory judgment allowed before a law is enforced)

POLITICAL QUESTIONS — nonjusticable issues committed to other branches of government (e.g., foreign affairs, Guaranty Clause issues, congressional membership requirements; but not apportionment of legislative districts)

11TH AMENDMENT — provides a state cannot be sued in federal court without consent; however, state officials may be sued for federal law violations; local governments can be sued; the United States or another state may sue a state; Congress can remove a state's immunity (e.g., for civil rights violations)

ABSTENTION — Pullman doctrine applies where a federal claim is based on an unsettled issue of state law; procedurally, the federal court retains jurisdiction of the federal claim
Younger doctrine prohibits review/enjoining of pending state criminal proceedings, criminally related civil proceedings, and civil contempt proceedings; procedurally the party is sent back to state court for all purposes

ADEQUATE AND INDEPENDENT STATE GROUNDS — The Supreme Court will not review a state decision based on a clear, adequate, independent and fully dispositive nonfederal ground

2. SEPARATION OF POWERS

Doctrine of Enumerated Powers

FEDERAL GOVERNMENT (FG) — has only that authority which the Constitution confers on it, either express or implied

10th AMENDMENT — powers not delegated to the FG are retained by the States under the 10th Amendment; under their police power, the States can legislate to protect any health, safety, welfare, morals, or aesthetics interest

NECESSARY AND PROPER CLAUSE — grants Congress the authority to carry into execution any enumerated power; not an independent source of power

Federal Legislative Power (Article 1, §8 Enumerated Powers)

COMMERCE POWER — plenary power which regulates both interstate and foreign commerce
Affectation Doctrine — regulates any activity whichhas a substantial economic effect on the stream of interstate commerce
Cumulative Impact Doctrine — even an entirely intrastate commercial or economic activity which has a cumulative impact on interstate commerce may be regulated

TAXING AND SPENDING POWER — plenary power to tax and spend for the general welfare; general welfare clause is not an independent source of power
Spending Power — Congress can attach strings to federal appropriations, thereby regulating indirectly where it cannot legislate directly
Taxing Power — a federal tax is valid if the dominant intent is fiscal; direct taxes (income tax) must be apportioned; indirectt axes (sales, use and excise taxes) must be geographically uniform

WAR POWER — to declare war, raise and support an army and navy, and make rules to regulate the armed forces; pervasive economic regulatory power during war; regulation maycontinue even after cessation of hostilities

OTHER ENUMERATED POWERS — postal power; power over District of Columbia; power to coin money; power to propose Constitutional amendments; immigration and naturalization; copyright, patent, bankruptcy powers; impeachment power

IMPLIED POWERS — broad investigatory power enforceable by contempt sanction; plenary admiralty power

Delegation of Legislative Power

LEGISLATIVE VETO — Congress can delegate its legislative power to executive and administrative agencies, but cannot subsequently retract it — such a "legislative veto" is unconstitutional (*INS v Chadha*)

(continued)

2. SEPARATION OF POWERS *(continued)*

Federal Executive Power (Article II)

DOMESTIC POLICY — Power and obligation to faithfully execute the laws

Appointment Powers — President can appoint purely executive officers (such as Cabinet members), ambassadors, public ministers, consuls and Supreme Court judges "with the advice and consent of the Senate"; Congress may not appoint members of bodies having administrative or enforcement powers, and may only appoint its legislative staff members; Congress can delegate appointment of "inferior officers" (such as a special prosecutor) to either the President, department heads, or the judiciary.

Removal Powers — the Constitution is silent; the President may remove purely executive officers (Cabinet members) without cause, but good cause is required to remove administrative officials with fixed terms of special need for independence from President; Congress has no power of summary removal

Veto Power — President has 10 days to exercise his veto, which may then be overridden by 2/3 vote of each house; President has no legislative power nor any power to impound funds

Pardon Power — extends only to federal crimes, not state crimes

Executive Privilege — to refuse to disclose information (military and diplomatic secrets); privilege must yield to important government interests

Absolute immunity in civil suits for damages based on actions taken while in office

FOREIGN POLICY — Commander in Chief of the Armed Forces — may establish military governments in occupied territories; broad emergency powers

Treaty Power — requires consent of 2/3 of the Senate.

Executive agreement — informal means by which the President can conduct day-to-day economic and business transactions between foreign countries without Senate consent

Foreign Affairs — President's power is not plenary, but is shared with Congress; sources of such power include: 1) Commander-in-chief; 2) Treaty Power; 3) Congressional Authorization (delegation by Congress of its commerce power to the President)

3. FEDERALISM (Federal limitations on state power)

STATE REGULATION OF THE FEDERAL GOVERNMENT — FG and its agencies are immune from state taxation and regulation; however, nondiscriminatory state taxes on federal contractors and employees are valid.

Intergovernmental Immunities

FEDERAL PROPERTY POWER (Art. IV, §3) — Congress may dispose of and make all needful rules and regulations respecting the territory or other property of the United States; generally applies to wild animals, federal buildings and enclaves, military ships and planes, Indian reservations

FEDERAL GOVERNMENT REGULATION OF THE STATES — states are not immune under 10th or 11th amendments (FG may sue a state; one state may sue another state); FG may tax proprietary state businesses

10TH AMENDMENT — powers not delegated to the FG, nor constitutionally prohibited to the states, are reserved to the states; a weak limitation on the federal commerce power; FG may not compel states (rather than private entities) to enact a particular regulatory program [e.g. regulate radioactive waste or take title to it — *N.Y. v U.S.*]

Dormant Commerce Clause

NEGATIVE IMPLICATIONS DOCTRINE — where Congress has not otherwise regulated, the states are free to regulate interstate commerce; regulation must be 1) non-discriminatory — may not favor or protect local interests, and 2) not unduly burdensome — state interest is balanced against the burden on interstate commerce such that no less restrictive alternative means is available

EXCEPTION — Market Participant Doctrine — where the state uses its own taxpayer funds to create the market, it may favor its own residents with subsidies and hiring preferences

COMPARE: Article IV Privileges and Immunities Clause — prevents discrimination by one state against citizens of another state regarding basic economic rights and liberties; N/A to corporations or aliens

State Taxation of Interstate Commerce

REQUIREMENTS: state tax must be reasonable and nondiscriminatory to satisfy the Commerce Clause, and a substantial nexus (more than "minimum contacts") must exist between the state interest and the activity being taxed to satisfy the Due Process Clause

GENERAL PRINCIPLES — goods or commodities "in the stream" of interstate commerce are exempt from state taxation, but may be taxed at the beginning and end of transit, as well as if there is a break in transit, Instrumentalities (cars, planes, trains, etc.) may be taxed provided the tax is fairly apportioned to the extent of taxpayer use (taxable situs requirement)

Supremacy Clause Article VI, §2

FIELD PREEMPTION — any state law in an area where Congress intends to occupy the field is unconstitutional (e.g., FAA, NLRB)

CONFLICT PREEMPTION — any state law in actual conflict with a federal law will be unconstitutional. Note: where federal law only establishes minimum standards, states may afford greater protection by enacting stricter laws than required by federal standards

4. PROTECTION OF INDIVIDUAL RIGHTS

Bill of Rights (the 1st 10 Amendments restrict the FG)

SELECTIVE INCORPORATION — under the 14th Amendment Due Process Clause, most Bill of Rights limitations are applicable to the states, except for a few provisions such as:

• 5th Amendment right to a grand jury in criminal cases

• 7th Amendment right to jury trial for civil cases

Retroactive Legislation

CONTRACTS CLAUSE — prevents the states (not the FG) from enacting legislation which retroactively impairs the obligation of either public or private contracts; usually, the state's police power "modification" argument prevails over the plaintiff's "impairment" argument

EX POST FACTO LAWS — make criminal conduct that was not a crime when committed, or increase the punishment for a crime after its commission, or decrease the amount of evidence needed to convict; such legislation which retroactively alters the criminal law is unconstitutional as applied to both the state and federal governments

BILL OF ATTAINDER — legislative punishment of a named group or individual without judicial trial; applies to both state and federal governments

KAPLAN pmbr

4. PROTECTION OF INDIVIDUAL RIGHTS *(continued)*

State Action

DEFINITION: a threshold requirement of government conduct which must be satisfied before discrimination can be restricted under the 14th or 15th Amendments; 13th Amendment can punish purely private acts of discrimination without showing state action

EXAMPLES OF STATE ACTION

PUBLIC FUNCTION — where a private entity is performing activities traditionally and exclusively carried on by the state (e.g., a company town)

COMPARE: NO PUBLIC FUNCTION — a privately owned utility company under heavy state regulation; operation of a nursing home

SIGNIFICANT STATE INVOLVEMENT — public school system; use of state-owned textbooks by a private school; "symbiotic relationship" or situation where the state facilities, encourages, or authorizes discrimination in areas such as housing, employment, or providing essential services

COMPARE: NO STATE ACTION — granting of a liquor license; private school discharging teachers; private school licensed by the state

Procedural Due Process

the procedural safeguards of NOTICE and a HEARING are available whenever there is a serious deprivation of any life, liberty or property interest

PROCEDURE — the court balances the severity of harm to the individual against the administrative costs of the government to determine what, if any, safeguards are required

PROTECTED LIBERTY INTERESTS — commitment to a mental institution; right to contract; right to engage in gainful employment; right to refuse unwanted medical care; right of natural parents in the care and custody of their children; not injury to reputation

PROPERTY INTERESTS (entitlements) — right to public education; welfare benefits; liability benefits; continued public employment where termination can only be "for cause"; revocation of a driver's license

(continued)

4. PROTECTION OF INDIVIDUAL RIGHTS *(continued)*

Takings — private property may not be taken for public use without just compensation; eminent domain and inverse condemnation require compensation, but exercise of state police power "regulation" does not

a per se taking consists of a confiscation (public easement granted across owner's beachfront property) or a physical occupation (cable TV wire installed in all the hallways of city rental units) or a regulation which denies the owner all reasonable economically viable use (post-purchase zoning ordinance which prohibits the owner from erecting any permanent structures on hisland); "balancing" test determines whether taking has occurred when there is no per se taking

Substantive Due Process

ECONOMIC REGULATION — regulation must meet rational basis scrutiny

FUNDAMENTAL RIGHTS — regulation must meet strict scrutiny standard

RIGHT TO VOTE OR BE CANDIDATE — other than for minimum age or residency requirements or payment of reasonable filing fees, regulation must meet the strict scrutiny standard. Generally voting districts for federal, state, and local elections are required to adhere very closely to the one person-one vote principle *(Reynolds v. Sims)*; exception for special limited-purpose districts (water storage district). Apportionment and districting schemes which distort voting districts for racial or political purposesis unconstitutional gerrymandering

RIGHT TO TRAVEL — durational residency requirements are invalid for receiving state medical care or welfare benefits, but valid for reduced tuition at state universities, obtaining a divorce, or registering to vote in a state primary election; foreign travelis subject only to rational basis scrutiny

RIGHT TO PRIVACY (mnemonic CAMPER) — Contraception — applies to the sale and use of contraceptives by both married and unmarried persons

Abortion — states may not prohibit abortions before viability, but may regulate as long as they create no "undue burden" on the right to obtain an abortion *(Planned Parenthood v. Casey)*; there is no right to abortion funding, even for indigents; consent of one or both parents or a judge, may be required for a minor to obtain an abortion

Marriage — any restriction on the right to marry (interracial marriage) is prohibited

Procreation — closely related to contraception

Education — right of parents to educate their children outside of public schools

Relations — right of related persons to live together; "anti-group" ordinances generally prohibited

5. EQUAL PROTECTION

an equal protection challenge arises where persons similarly situated are treated differently

3 Standards of Review

STRICT SCRUTINY — burden on the state to show the law is necessary (i.e. no less restrictive alternative means exists) to a compelling interest; applies to 3 areas:

(regulation unlikely to succeed)

1. Protected 1st Amendment Rights

2. Suspect Classes (mnemonic RAN)

— **Race** — purposeful discrimination required; race-based affirmative action plans are subject to strict scrutiny whether passed by the state *(Richmond v Croson)* or by the federal government *(Adarand Construction v Pena)*

— **Alienage** — federal regulation is subject only to rational basis scrutiny, whereas state regulation is subject to strict scrutiny, except where participation in government (policemen, teachers, serving on a jury list) is involved; illegal aliens are not suspect

— **National Origin**

3. Fundamental Rights — Right to Vote
— Right to Travel
— Right to Privacy

Middle-tier (Intermediate) Scrutiny — burden on the state to show the law is substantially related to an important interest, applies to 2 areas:

1. Gender
2. Illegitimacy
— purposeful discrimination required; affirmative action permitted subject to middle-tier test

Rational Basis Scrutiny — burden is on plaintiff to show the law is not rationally related to any legitimate interest; applies to all other classifications including 1. Poverty 2. Age 3. Mental Retardation 4. Necessities of life (food, shelter, clothing, medical care) 5. Economic and social welfare measures

(regulation likely to succeed)

6. FIRST AMENDMENT GUARANTEES

Freedom of Religion

FREE EXERCISE CLAUSE – an individual's religious beliefs are absolutely protected; conduct in furtherance of those beliefs may be regulated; a law that discriminates against a person's religious conduct is subject to a strict scrutiny, but no special accommodations for religious conduct are required where a law is neutral and generally applicable; e.g., use of peyote during religious ceremonies is conduct which may be prohibited despite the individual's religious beliefs which required this practice *(Oregon v Smith)*; a Jewish soldier may be compelled by the Air Force not to wear his yarmulke as part of his military uniform *(Goldman v Weinberger)*

ESTABLISHMENT CLAUSE – Main Principle: the government may not aid or prefer one religion or secto ver another, subject to strict scrutiny review;
—Test: to be constitutional, a sect-neutral government aid/program musts atisfy 3 requirementsu nder the *Lemon* test — the law must 1) have a secular purpose; 2) have a primary effect that neither advances nor inhibits religion, and 3) not foster excessive government entanglementw ith religion
— General Principles: government sponsored religious activities in public schools are unconstitutional (dailyB ible readings; a moment of silent, voluntary prayer; prohibition of the teaching of evolution); government aid to parochial schools may not be used for religious purposes (use of textbooks, busing, health tests), but such aid is constitutional if made available to all students at public and private schools
—Tax Deduction – reimbursing parents for tuition paid only to *religious* schools is invalid; similarly,t ax exemptions available only for religious organizations (no sales tax for religious publications)i s an invalid endorsement of religion, but propertyt ax exemptions for religious propertyh ave been upheld; religious displays (nativity scenes; menorahs) are permissible in public places provided no one religion is being favored over another

6. FIRST AMENDMENT GUARANTEES *(continued)*

Freedom of Speech Approach

4 TYPES OF FACIAL ATTACKS — Overbreadth — statute punishes both protected as well as unprotected speech

Vagueness — statute is so unclearly defined that persons of ordinary intelligence must guess at its meaning

Prior Restraint — government action restricting free speech in advance of publication is generally invalid (licensing permits, injunctions; 'gag' order barring the media from pretrial publicity); valid where national security interests are compelling, or for the regulation of obscene books and films where procedural safeguards are afforded

Unfettered Discretion — where a licensing official has unfettered discretion as to whether to confer or deny a permit

ESSAY APPROACH

Track One — Ask: Is the Government's Action **Content Specific** (regulates the message)

If content specific, then ask: Is the speech being regulated **Protected** or **Unprotected**

If "protected" then apply strict scrutiny i.e. — the statute is unconstitutional unless the government can show the law is necessary to a compelling interest

Unprotected includes clear and present danger; defamation; obscenity; child pornography; fighting words; fraudulent commercial speech

or

Track Two — **Content Neutral** — Time, Place, or Manner Regulation (regulation does not depend on the speaker's identity, message, or viewpoint)

If content neutral regulation of time, place, manner, then apply a 3-part test: the regulation must

1) further a significant government interest (e.g., noise, crowd, or litter control; traffic safety)
2) be narrowly tailored (no more restrictive than necessary), and
3) leave open alternative channels of communication (e.g., commercial door-to-door solicitation without invitation of the homeowner may be restricted because other avenues of communication exist such as the mail, newspaper advertisements, radio and television)

(continued)

6. FIRST AMENDMENT GUARANTEES *(continued)*

Freedom of Association — unmentioned First Amendment right encompassing activities such as accepting government benefits, public employment or seeking membership in various organizations

Public Employment and Bar Membership — may not be denied based upon an individual's group affiliation unless the government can show the person 1) is a knowing (scienter) and active (dues-paying) member of a subversive group and 2) has the specific intent to further the group's unlawful objectives *(Keyishian v Bd. of Rights)*

Loyalty Oaths — generally *invalid* as a condition to public employment, however, an oath to support the Constitution and oppose overthrow of the government has been upheld *(Cole v Richardson)*

Disclosure Requirements — to avoid a chilling effect on First Amendment activities disclosure is generally not required, unless the government could make such membership illegal

Freedom of the Press — read together with the "free speech" clause as a single guarantee; generally the press has no greater privilege than the ordinary citizen

Right of Access — both the public and the press have a right to attend a criminal trial, which may be outweighed by an overriding government interest

Newsperson's Privilege — no privilege exists to refuse to disclose confidential sources to a grand jury *(Branzburg v Hayes)*, but states may enact "shield" laws to afford such protection

Broadcasting — may be regulated more closely than the press due to the limited number of frequencies available — "equal time" broadcasts may be required *(Red Lion)*, yet on the other hand a newspaper need not provide equal space for political rebuttal *(Miami Herald)*

6. FIRST AMENDMENT GUARANTEES *(continued)*

Freedom of Speech Content — most forms of speech are protected subject to the strict scrutiny standard; 6 forms of unprotected speech may be regulated

CLEAR AND PRESENT DANGER — speech 1) directed at producing imminent unlawful action and 2) likely to produce such action *(Brandenburg v Ohio)*

DEFAMATION — public officials, public figures, and limited public figures (those who voluntarily inject themselves in the limelight) must prove malice: knowing falsity or reckless disregard for the truth *(Times v Sullivan)* — private person plaintiffs — constitutional limitations apply only where the defamatory statement involves a matter of public concern, in which case negligence must be proven (no liability without fault); punitive damages are not awarded absent proof of malice *(Gertz v Welch)*

OBSCENITY — to be obscene, the speech must 1) appeal to the prurient interest in sex applying contemporary community standards, 2) depict sexual conduct in a patently offensive way, and 3) lack serious literary, artistic, political, or scientific value *(Miller v California)* — merely offensive language is not obscene; however, profane language on the airways may be restricted *(Pacifica Foundation)*; private possession of obscene materials in one's home is protected (except for child pornography), although viewing, sale and distribution of such obscene material may be vigorously regulated (movie ratings, zoning ordinances)

CHILD PORNOGRAPHY — outside the protection of the First Amendment; visual depictions of sexual conduct including children may be punished even if not "obscene" under *Miller (N.Y. v Ferber)*

FIGHTING WORDS — restricted speech includes personally abrasive language likely to incite the average person to commit acts of physical violence *(Chaplinsky v N.H.)*; however, statutes designed to punish only particular viewpoints are invalid — e.g. fighting words that provoke violence on the basis of race, religion, or gender *(R.A.V. v St. Paul)*

FRAUDULENT COMMERCIAL SPEECH — generally commercial speech is protected but may be restricted as to false or deceptive advertising or illegal products; a lawful, narrowly tailored regulation will be valid if it directly advances a substantial government interest and there is a reasonable "fit" between the means used and the legislation's end *(Central Hudson; SUNY v Fox)*; attorneys may advertise, provided it is not misleading; in-person solicitation for profit is not protected.

OTHER AREAS — symbolic speech (where the medium itself is the message) may be restricted where the regulation furthers an important government interest unrelated to the suppression of speech and the incidental burden on speech is no greater than necessary; e.g., unconstitutional to ban flag burning *(U.S. v Eichman)* — freedom not to speak — allows children not to be compelled to salute or pledge allegiance to the American flag, and allows a motorist to cover the motto ("Live Free or Die") portion of her license plate

(continued)

6. FIRST AMENDMENT GUARANTEES *(continued)*

Time, Place, Manner Restrictions

reasonable restriction of speech conduct is permitted by means of content-neutral time, place, manner regulations

PUBLIC FORUMS — (streets, parks, sidewalks) — regulations must satisfy 3-part test (See Track Two test on previous page)

NONPUBLIC FORUMS — (jails, military bases, mailboxes, billboards, public buses, government buildings, airport terminals)

— to be valid the regulations must be 1) viewpoint neutral (i.e., content may be regulated, but limiting the presentation to only one view is impermissible) and 2) reasonably related to a legitimate government interest

Licensing Statutes

REQUIREMENTS — to be valid, a licensing scheme must relate to an important government objective, be clearly written, narrowly drawn, and reasonably regulate time, place and manner of speech

IF STATUTE IS VALID ON ITS FACE — the speaker may not ignore the statute and must seek a permit. If the request is denied, even wrongfully, the speaker must nonetheless seek prompt judicial relief before speaking; otherwise a subsequent claim of violation of 1st Amendment rights will fail

IF STATUTE IS VOID ON ITS FACE — due to overbreadth, vagueness, prior restraint, or unfettered discretion — the speaker may ignore the statute and speak, as well as successfully defend against any subsequent prosecution (*Shuttlesworth v Birmingham*)

IF AN INJUNCTION IS ISSUED — where the speaker is enjoined from speaking, she must obey the injunction (even if it is facially invalid) or appeal from it. Invalidity of the injunction must be established on appeal and is no defense to a subsequent charge of contempt (*Walker v Birmingham*)

1. OFFER AND ACCEPTANCE

O = Offeror   E = Offeree   K = Contract

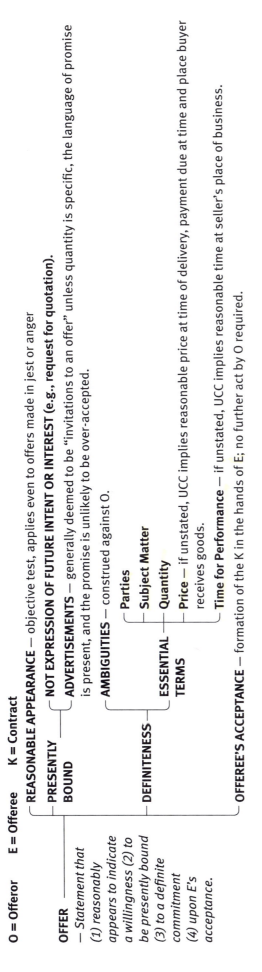

OFFER — Statement that (1) reasonably appears to indicate a willingness (2) to be presently bound (3) to a definite commitment (4) upon E's acceptance.

PRESENTLY BOUND

- **REASONABLE APPEARANCE** — objective test, applies even to offers made in jest or anger
- **NOT EXPRESSION OF FUTURE INTENT OR INTEREST (e.g., request for quotation).**
- **ADVERTISEMENTS** — generally deemed to be "invitations to an offer" unless quantity is specific, the language of promise is present, and the promise is unlikely to be over-accepted.

DEFINITENESS

- **AMBIGUITIES** — construed against O.
- **ESSENTIAL TERMS**
  - **Parties**
  - **Subject Matter**
  - **Quantity**
  - **Price** — if unstated, UCC implies reasonable price at time of delivery, payment due at time and place buyer receives goods.
  - **Time for Performance** — if unstated, UCC implies reasonable time at seller's place of business.

OFFEREE'S ACCEPTANCE — formation of the K in the hands of E; no further act by O required.

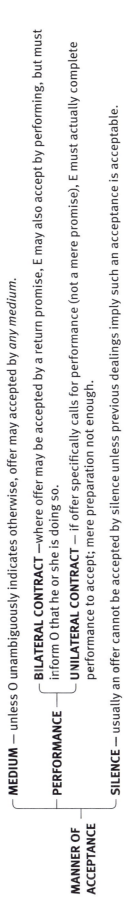

MANNER OF ACCEPTANCE

- **MEDIUM** — unless O unambiguously indicates otherwise, offer may accepted by *any medium.*
- **PERFORMANCE**
  - **BILATERAL CONTRACT** — where offer may be accepted by a return promise, E may also accept by performing, but must inform O that he or she is doing so.
  - **UNILATERAL CONTRACT** — if offer specifically calls for performance (not a mere promise), E must actually complete performance to accept; mere preparation not enough.
- **SILENCE** — usually an offer cannot be accepted by silence unless previous dealings imply such an acceptance is acceptable.

(continued)

1. OFFER AND ACCEPTANCE (continued)

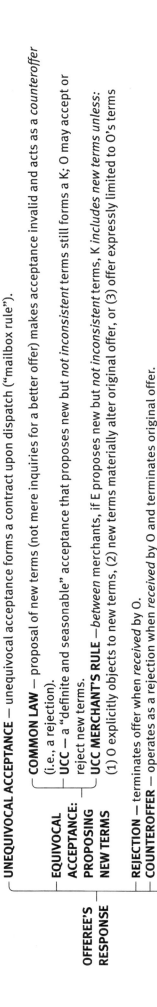

OFFEREE'S RESPONSE

UNEQUIVOCAL ACCEPTANCE — unequivocal acceptance forms a contract upon dispatch ("mailbox rule").

EQUIVOCAL ACCEPTANCE: PROPOSING NEW TERMS

- **COMMON LAW** — proposal of new terms (not mere inquiries for a better offer) makes acceptance invalid and acts as a *counteroffer* (i.e., a rejection).
- **UCC** — a "definite and seasonable" acceptance that proposes new but *not inconsistent* terms still forms a K; O may accept or reject new terms.
- **UCC MERCHANT'S RULE** —*between* merchants, if E proposes new but *not inconsistent* terms, K *includes new terms unless:* (1) O explicitly objects to new terms, (2) new terms materially alter original offer, or (3) offer expressly limited to O's terms

REJECTION — terminates offer when *received* by O.

COUNTEROFFER — operates as a rejection when *received* by O and terminates original offer.

INDECISION — offer remains open until terminated by O or lapse of time.

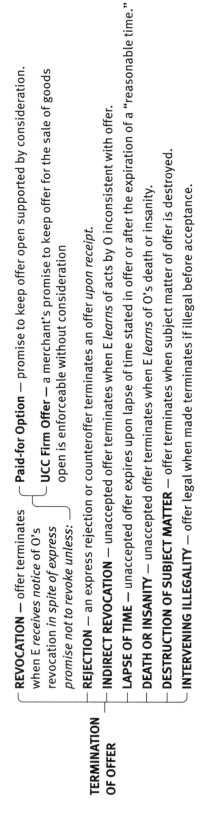

TERMINATION OF OFFER

REVOCATION — offer terminates when E *receives notice* of O's revocation *in spite of express promise not to revoke unless:*

- **Paid-for Option** — promise to keep offer open supported by consideration.
- **UCC Firm Offer** — a merchant's promise to keep offer for the sale of goods open is enforceable without consideration

REJECTION — an express rejection or counteroffer terminates an offer *upon receipt.*

INDIRECT REVOCATION — unaccepted offer terminates when E *learns* of acts by O inconsistent with offer.

LAPSE OF TIME — unaccepted offer expires upon lapse of time stated in offer or after the expiration of a "reasonable time."

DEATH OR INSANITY — unaccepted offer terminates when E *learns* of O's death or insanity.

DESTRUCTION OF SUBJECT MATTER — offer terminates when subject matter of offer is destroyed.

INTERVENING ILLEGALITY — offer legal when made terminates if illegal before acceptance.

2. THIRD-PARTY BENEFICIARIES

DEFINITIONS

Promissee-Benefactor (X) ⟵ **Promisor (Y)**

Third-Party Beneficiary (Z)

ISSUE SPOTTING SEQUENCE

THIRD-PARTY BENEFICIARIES:
Contractual rights created in a third person at the time of formation:

STATUS OF BENEFICIARY
What was the parties' intent with regard to any benefit conferred upon Z?

- **INCIDENTAL BENEFICIARY** — if the parties had no specific intent or motive to confer a benefit on Z.
- **DONEE BENEFICIARY** — if the parties intended to confer a gratuitous gift on Z.
- **CREDITOR BENEFICIARY** — if the parties intended to confer a benefit on Z to satisfy a pre-existing debt or obligation.

RIGHTS OF BENEFICIARY
If a party fails to perform, what rights does Z have?

- **INCIDENTAL BENEFICIARY** — no rights against either Y or X.

- **DONEE BENEFICIARY**
  — Z's rights *vest* upon knowledge of X-Y contract (some states require reliance)
  - **Against Y** — Z stands in shoes of X in suit against Y.
  - **Against X** — Z may prevent X from rescinding X-Y contract but may not sue X if Y fails to perform.

- **CREDITOR BENEFICIARY**
  — Z's rights vest upon his reliance on X-Y contract.
  - **Against Y** — Z stands in shoes of X in suit against Y.
  - **Against X** — Z may sue X on original obligation, disregarding X-Y contract (unless there was a novation).

3. CONTRACT REMEDIES

Restitution — recovery of money already paid to breaching party (less possible *quantum meruit* offset).

Reliance Costs — recovery of out-of-pocket expenses in preparing to perform.

Incidental Costs — recovery of costs necessitated by breach directly relating to the contract itself (e.g., shipping, storage, inspection, reselling or repurchasing).

MONEY DAMAGES — normal remedy; should place non-breaching party in position he or she would have been in had the contract been performed.

Expected Bargained-For Benefit — *not* including anticipated profits (see consequential costs).

SALES CONTRACTS — difference between the market price at the time of breach and the contract price.

SERVICE CONTRACT
- **Employee** — full contract price *if* he or she has performed or stands ready to do so (*less* mitigation).
- **Employer** — recovery limited to costs of replacement.

Consequential Costs and Losses — money damages resulting from special situation of non-breaching party (*not* including mental anguish or inconvenience).

FORESEEABLE — reasonably foreseeable costs and losses contemplated by both parties at the time of the contract may be recovered.

MITIGATION — non-breaching party's recovery must be reduced if he or she fails to take reasonable efforts to reduce costs of breach.

Liquidated Damages — contractual provision setting the total amount of all money damages in the event of breach

REASONABLE AMOUNT — amount must be reasonable in light of parties' contemplations at the time of contract.

NECESSARY — amount of actual damages must be difficult to ascertain.

TAILORED TO CONTRACT — provision must be tailored to nature of contract (i.e., *not* boilerplate).

Punitive Damages — only available in extreme cases of malicious or intentional breach (like a separate tort recovery).

KAPLAN) *pmbr*

3. CONTRACT REMEDIES *(continued)*

SPECIFIC PERFORMANCE
— court may order breaching party to perform the contract.

- **Contract Must be Valid and Enforceable**
- **Money Damages Must Be Inadequate**
  - **UNIQUE SUBJECT MATTER** — land, stock of close corporation, one-of-a-kind item.
  - **AMOUNT NOT ASCERTAINABLE**
- **No Special Problems of Enforcement** — (e.g., personal service contract may *not* be specifically enforced).

RESCISSION
— cancellation of the contract to put parties as they were before the contract.

- **Grounds**
  - **MUTUAL MISTAKE IN FORMATION**
  - **FRAUD** — knowing misrepresentation of material fact relied upon by non-breaching party.
  - **MAJOR BREACH CHANGING NATURE OF AGREEMENT**
- **Requirements**
  - **NOTIFICATION WITHIN REASONABLE TIME**
  - **RESTORATION OF NON-BREACHING PARTY TO STATUS QUO** *—non-breaching party* must return all consideration unless alteration or change made in good faith reliance that breaching party would perform.

REFORMATION — court may reform contract to accurately describe the actual agreement if there was a mutual mistake.

QUASI-CONTRACT — an alternative theory for money damages based on equity rather than contract.

1. FORMATION AND OTHER THRESHOLD CONCEPTS

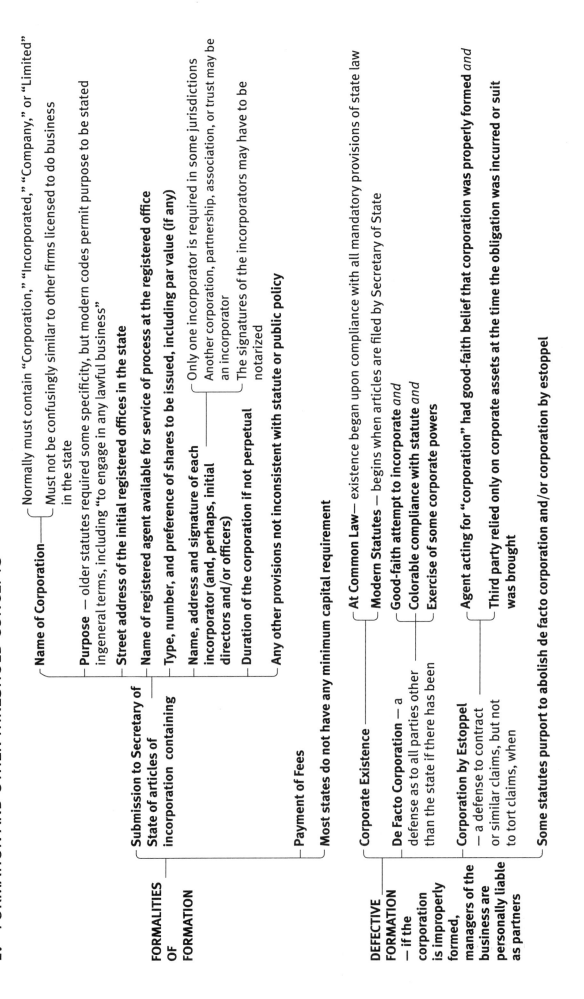

FORMALITIES OF FORMATION

- **Submission to Secretary of State of articles of incorporation containing**
  - **Name of Corporation**
    - Normally must contain "Corporation," "Incorporated," "Company," or "Limited"
    - Must not be confusingly similar to other firms licensed to do business in the state
  - **Purpose** — older statutes required some specificity, but modern codes permit purpose to be stated in general terms, including "to engage in any lawful business"
  - **Street address of the initial registered offices in the state**
  - **Name of registered agent available for service of process at the registered office**
  - **Type, number, and preference of shares to be issued, including par value (if any)**
  - **Name, address and signature of each incorporator (and, perhaps, initial directors and/or officers)**
    - Only one incorporator is required in some jurisdictions
    - Another corporation, partnership, association, or trust may be an incorporator
    - The signatures of the incorporators may have to be notarized
  - **Duration of the corporation if not perpetual**
  - **Any other provisions not inconsistent with statute or public policy**
- **Payment of Fees**
- **Most states do not have any minimum capital requirement**

DEFECTIVE FORMATION — if the corporation is improperly formed, managers of the business are personally liable as partners

- **Corporate Existence**
  - **At Common Law** — existence began upon compliance with all mandatory provisions of state law
  - **Modern Statutes** — begins when articles are filed by Secretary of State
- **De Facto Corporation** — a defense as to all parties other than the state if there has been
  - Good-faith attempt to incorporate *and*
  - Colorable compliance with statute *and*
  - Exercise of some corporate powers
- **Corporation by Estoppel** — a defense to contract or similar claims, but not to tort claims, when
  - Agent acting for "corporation" had good-faith belief that corporation was properly formed *and*
  - Third party relied only on corporate assets at the time the obligation was incurred or suit was brought
- **Some statutes purport to abolish de facto corporation and/or corporation by estoppel**

1. FORMATION AND OTHER THRESHOLD CONCEPTS *(continued)*

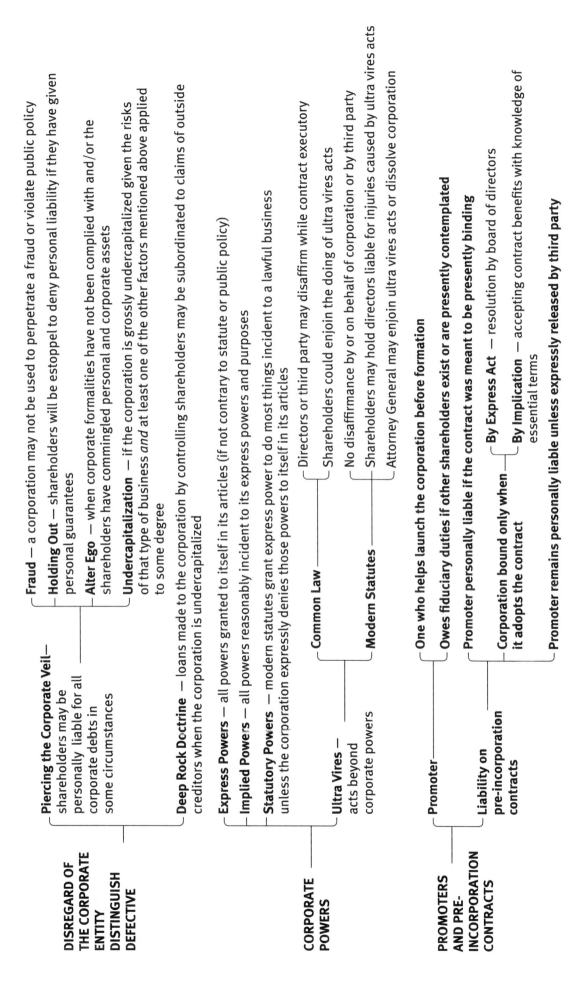

DISREGARD OF THE CORPORATE ENTITY

DISTINGUISH DEFECTIVE

Piercing the Corporate Veil — shareholders may be personally liable for all corporate debts in some circumstances

- **Fraud** — a corporation may not be used to perpetrate a fraud or violate public policy
- **Holding Out** — shareholders will be estoppel to deny personal liability if they have given personal guarantees
- **Alter Ego** — when corporate formalities have not been complied with and/or the shareholders have commingled personal and corporate assets
- **Undercapitalization** — if the corporation is grossly undercapitalized given the risks of that type of business *and* at least one of the other factors mentioned above applied to some degree

Deep Rock Doctrine — loans made to the corporation by controlling shareholders may be subordinated to claims of outside creditors when the corporation is undercapitalized

CORPORATE POWERS

- **Express Powers** — all powers granted to itself in its articles (if not contrary to statute or public policy)
- **Implied Powers** — all powers reasonably incident to its express powers and purposes
- **Statutory Powers** — modern statutes grant express power to do most things incident to a lawful business unless the corporation expressly denies those powers to itself in its articles

Ultra Vires — acts beyond corporate powers

Common Law
- Directors or third party may disaffirm while contract executory
- Shareholders could enjoin the doing of ultra vires acts

Modern Statutes
- No disaffirmance by or on behalf of corporation or by third party
- Shareholders may hold directors liable for injuries caused by ultra vires acts
- Attorney General may enjoin ultra vires acts or dissolve corporation

PROMOTERS AND PRE-INCORPORATION CONTRACTS

Promoter
- One who helps launch the corporation before formation
- Owes fiduciary duties if other shareholders exist or are presently contemplated

Liability on pre-incorporation contracts
- Promoter personally liable if the contract was meant to be presently binding
- Corporation bound only when it adopts the contract
  - **By Express Act** — resolution by board of directors
  - **By Implication** — accepting contract benefits with knowledge of essential terms
- Promoter remains personally liable unless expressly released by third party

2a. SHAREHOLDERS

RIGHTS AND POWERS

- Elect and remove directors
- Approve fundamental changes (e.g., amendments to articles, mergers, consolidations, sales of all or substantially all assets, voluntary dissolution)
  - Some states provide for *absolute* right to certain records if shareholder owns a specified percentage of the outstanding shares and/or has been a shareholder for specified time
  - *Any* shareholder may obtain court order after showing proper purpose
  - **Denial of Right** — corporate secretary may deny inspection if shareholder is acting for improper purpose or in bad faith; if right improperly denied, shareholder may obtain writ of mandamus *and* may be entitled to damages
- Right to inspect shareholder lists and other corporate book records
- Make and amend bylaws
- Right to receive dividends and, upon dissolution, pro rata share of assets remaining after creditors are paid
- Any other rights or powers reserved to shareholders in the articles

MEETINGS

- **Annual Meeting**
  - **Notice**
    - **Purpose** — statutes vary on how much detail notice must give as to business to be conducted; generally must be told beforehand if they will be asked to approve fundamental changes
    - **Time and Place** — must always be given within designated window (i.e., not less than 10 nor more than 60 days before meeting)
  - **Quorum** — majority of shares entitled to vote unless the articles or bylaws provide otherwise

- **Special Meetings** — may be called by the board or others so authorized by articles or bylaws
  - **Notice** — same as annual meeting, but *must* always state purpose of the meeting and only that business may be conducted
  - **Quorum** — same as annual meeting

- **Action without Meeting** — in some states, any shareholder action may be taken without a meeting *if* the required number of shares consents in writing. Notice of the action must be given to all shareholders who did not consent

2a. SHAREHOLDERS *(continued)*

VOTING

Election of Directors — candidates who receive highest number of votes cast are elected (i.e., election requires *plurality*, not majority)

- **Straight Line Voting** — majority bloc elects entire board
- **Cumulative Voting** — directors may be elected by cumulative voting, whereby each shareholder has a number of votes equal to the number of shares she owns times the number of directors to be elected, which may all be voted for one or more candidates, thus giving minority shareholders an opportunity to obtain some representation on the board

Other Transactions — require approval by simple majority in most states unless articles or bylaws call for a higher vote

- **Fundamental Changes** — approval of fundamental changes requires *majority of all shares entitled to vote*
- **Other Actions** — require approval of majority present at a valid meeting at which a quorum is present (but see **Action without Meeting**, above)

PROXIES — written grant of right to vote shareholder's stock

Term — generally valid only for 11 months unless proxy expressly provides for longer term

Revocation — normally, proxies may be revoked notwithstanding promise not to do; they are revoked by:
- Express revocation by shareholder
- Death or incompetence of shareholder (but only when corporation receives notice)
- Subsequent proxy
- Transfer of stock to taker without knowledge

Irrevocable Proxies — proxies are irrevocable for a specified time if proxy so provides and proxy is coupled with an interest; look for relationship of:
- Lender to corporation
- Employee of corporation
- Purchaser and seller of stock
- Pledgor and pledgee
- Stock subject to shareholder agreement

Proxy Solicitations — see Flowchart 2d

SHAREHOLDER AGREEMENTS

Vote Pooling Agreement — a written agreement between shareholders that they will vote in a certain way; normally enforced by an order of specific performance

Voting Trust — actual transfer of ownership to a trustee who has power to vote stock; normally such agreements are not valid for more than 10 years

Management Agreement — written agreements concerning management of business are enforceable if all shareholders assent

2b. DIRECTORS

POWERS AND OBLIGATIONS OF BOARD OF DIRECTORS
— must use their unfettered discretion in managing the business

- May not improperly delegate decision-making powers
  - **Scope** — must not delegate too much authority (even to an Executive Committee)
  - **Time** — delegations for too long a time are void
  - **Reviewability** — the less power the board has retained to overrule or discharge the delegatee the less likely the delegation will be valid
- Select, supervise, and remove officers and other agents
- Make and amend bylaws if articles so provide
- Declare dividends
- Fill vacancies of the board by majority vote of the remaining directors
- Initiate procedures for fundamental changes (e.g., mergers and consolidations)
- Incur and settle corporate debts
- Buy and sell corporate property and stock

ELECTION AND REMOVAL OF DIRECTORS

- No special requirements unless articles or bylaws so provide
- Directors are elected annually (except in the case of staggered directors [see below])
- Board may be staggered so that not all directors are elected annually
- Articles may grant each class the right to elect one or more directors
- Removal
  - **General Rule** — by majority vote of shareholders entitled to vote for directors with or without cause (but see cumulative voting limitation on JIG 2a)
  - In some states, directors may be removed for cause by other directors
  - By court upon a showing of gross abuse of position

KAPLAN pmbr

2b. DIRECTORS (continued)

MEETINGS

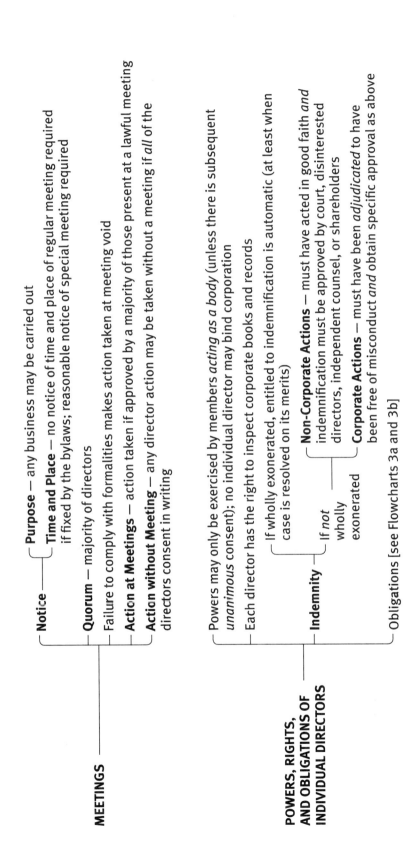

Notice
- **Purpose** — any business may be carried out
- **Time and Place** — no notice of time and place of regular meeting required if fixed by the bylaws; reasonable notice of special meeting required

Quorum — majority of directors

Failure to comply with formalities makes action taken at meeting void

Action at Meetings — action taken if approved by a majority of those present at a lawful meeting

Action without Meeting — any director action may be taken without a meeting if *all* of the directors consent in writing

POWERS, RIGHTS, AND OBLIGATIONS OF INDIVIDUAL DIRECTORS

Powers may only be exercised by members *acting as a body* (unless there is subsequent *unanimous* consent); no individual director may bind corporation

Each director has the right to inspect corporate books and records

Indemnity
- If wholly exonerated, entitled to indemnification is automatic (at least when case is resolved on its merits)
- If *not* wholly exonerated
  - **Non-Corporate Actions** — must have acted in good faith *and* indemnification must be approved by court, disinterested directors, independent counsel, or shareholders
  - **Corporate Actions** — must have been *adjudicated* to have been free of misconduct *and* obtain specific approval as above

Obligations [see Flowcharts 3a and 3b]

KAPLAN) pmbr

2c. OFFICERS AND AGENTS

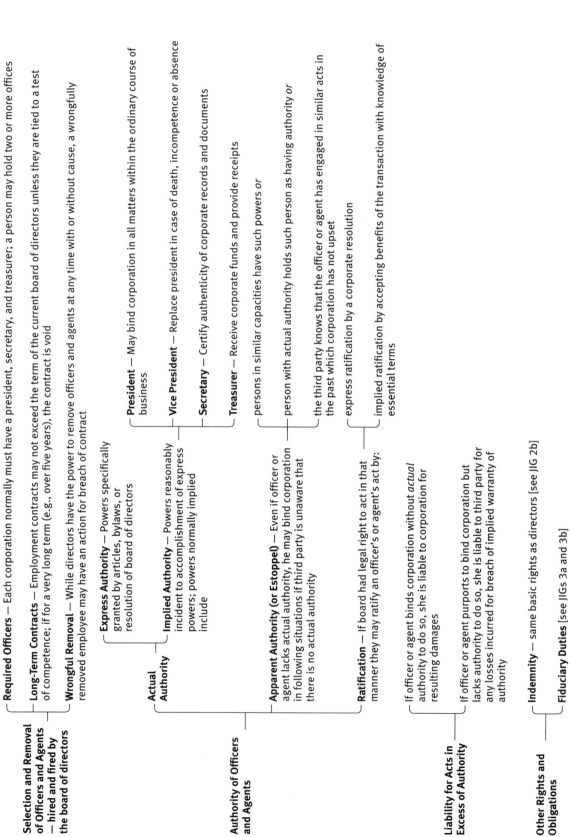

Selection and Removal of Officers and Agents — hired and fired by the board of directors

- **Required Officers** — Each corporation normally must have a president, secretary, and treasurer; a person may hold two or more offices
- **Long-Term Contracts** — Employment contracts may not exceed the term of the current board of directors unless they are tied to a test of competence; if for a very long term (e.g., over five years), the contract is void
- **Wrongful Removal** — While directors have the power to remove officers and agents at any time with or without cause, a wrongfully removed employee may have an action for breach of contract

Actual Authority
- **Express Authority** — Powers specifically granted by articles, bylaws, or resolution of board of directors
- **Implied Authority** — Powers reasonably incident to accomplishment of express powers; powers normally implied include
  - **President** — May bind corporation in all matters within the ordinary course of business
  - **Vice President** — Replace president in case of death, incompetence or absence
  - **Secretary** — Certify authenticity of corporate records and documents
  - **Treasurer** — Receive corporate funds and provide receipts

Authority of Officers and Agents

- **Apparent Authority (or Estoppel)** — Even if officer or agent lacks actual authority, he may bind corporation in following situations if third party is unaware that there is no actual authority
  - persons in similar capacities have such powers *or*
  - person with actual authority holds such person as having authority *or*
  - the third party knows that the officer or agent has engaged in similar acts in the past which corporation has not upset
- **Ratification** — If board had legal right to act in that manner they may ratify an officer's or agent's act by:
  - express ratification by a corporate resolution
  - implied ratification by accepting benefits of the transaction with knowledge of essential terms

Liability for Acts in Excess of Authority
- If officer or agent binds corporation without *actual* authority to do so, she is liable to corporation for resulting damages
- If officer or agent purports to bind corporation but lacks authority to do so, she is liable to third party for any losses incurred for breach of implied warranty of authority

Other Rights and Obligations
- **Indemnity** — same basic rights as directors [see JIG 2b]
- **Fiduciary Duties** [see JIGs 3a and 3b]

2d. PROXY SOLICITATIONS

STATE LAW
- **Common Law** — proxies obtained by fraud were void; solicitation is fraudulent only if plaintiff establishes that shareholders *would* be affected by error
- **Modern Trend** — considers whether the misstatement or omission was material as determined under Section 14(a) (see below)

SECTION 14(a) — solicitations by management or, if 10 or more shareholders are solicited, by non-management by use of an instrumentality of interstate commerce

- **Jurisdictional Requirement**
  - Stock listed on a national securities exchange *or*
  - Corporation which
    - Has 500 or more shareholders *and*
    - Has more than $3,000,000 in assets *and*
    - Is engaged in interstate commerce or whose stock is traded in interstate commerce

- **Must be Free of Omissions and Misstatements of Material Fact**
  - Materiality — fact is material if it is substantially likely to be considered
  - Reliance normally will be presumed
  - Prospective relief is usually granted irrespective of an improper mental state; retrospective relief normally granted if there was at least negligence

- **Solicitation Defined** — any communication with shareholders if it is part of a continuous plan intended to end with a request for a grant of a proxy

- **Proxy statement must accompany request for proxies and must be filed with SEC before distribution to shareholders**

- **Effect of Improper Solicitation**
  - Prospective Relief — if proxies not yet voted, court will enjoin the use of the proxies obtained
  - Retrospective Relief — If proxies already voted, court may void action taken or order new vote
  - Attempt to Get Proxies for Selves — can compel management to mail request (at dissident's expense) or include request with management's material (option belongs to the corporation)

- **Dissident's Rights (exist only when management is soliciting proxies)**
  - Submission of Proposals — shareholders may submit proposals to be included with management's solicitation; proposals may be excluded on the following grounds:
    - Beyond shareholders' powers
    - Personal grievances
    - Matters beyond corporation's control
    - Relates to selection or removal of directors
    - Opposes management's proposal
    - Received less than 3% of vote at recent shareholder meeting

WHO BEARS EXPENSE — only reasonable expenses may be charged to corporation
- **Management's Expenses** — directly borne by corporation so long as battle was in "the best interests of the corporation" (i.e., fight concerned fundamental corporate policy or was waged to prevent take-over by a corporate looter)
- **Insurgent's Rights** — may be reimbursed by corporation if
  - They succeed *and*
  - They acted in the best interests of the corporation *and*
  - Shareholders approve reimbursement

3a. FIDUCIARY OBLIGATIONS TO THE CORPORATION

COMMON LAW FIDUCIARY DUTIES OF DIRECTORS AND OFFICERS

- **DUTY OF GOOD FAITH (Loyalty)** — must act in best interests of corporation, not for personal gain

- **DUTY OF DUE CARE (Reasonableness)** — must exercise the degree of diligence, care and skill which the ordinary prudent person would be expected to exercise under similar circumstances

  - **Ordinary Situations (Business Judgment Rule)** — strong presumption directors not liable for losses based on a good-faith business judgment arrived at through the exercise of due care

APPLICATION TO SPECIAL SITUATIONS

- **Duty of Loyalty Problems**

  - Contracts with interested directors not voidable if in good faith and:
    - Disclosure of all material facts and approval of
      - Majority of board (disregarding vote of interested directors) *or*
      - Majority of shares
    - Contract is objectively fair

  - **Compensation of Directors** — must be reasonable, but need not be ratified by shareholders

  - **Retention of Control** — directors may use corporate assets to retain their positions only if necessary to
    - Protect basic policy
    - Prevent takeover by looter

  - **Usurpation of Corporate Opportunity** — may not make personal acquisition without first offering it to corporation if corporation had interest or expectancy in the property and financial means to acquire it

- **Duty of Due Care Problems**

  - **General Test** — must not buy at price above fair market value or sell at price below fair market value

  - **Compensation of Agents** — compensation (including retirement and stock option plans) must be reasonable considering benefits provided to corporation

  - **Knowledge**
    - Actual Knowledge — must utilize any information actually known, including special expertise
    - Implied Knowledge — presumed to know that which a person in a like position knows
    - Imputed Knowledge — presumed to know things known by other directors, officers, or agents

  - **Reliance on Others** — May rely on reports of employees, accountants, attorneys, etc., so long as such person is reasonably believed to be reliable and competent

FIDUCIARY OBLIGATIONS OF CONTROLLING SHAREHOLDERS — "Control" means the ability to elect or control a majority of the board of directors (does not necessarily require ownership of majority of shares)

- **General Obligation** — cannot obtain an *exclusive* benefit at the expense of the minority or creditors

- **Disposing of Control** — may sell control at a premium (i.e., at a price above the fair market value of the share) and keep that premium unless:
  - He knows or has reason to know that purchaser will harm the corporation, or
  - But for the sale of control, the minority shareholders would have shared in the premium

- **Sale of Corporate Office** — seller may have his directors resign and elect purchaser's nominees pursuant to sale of a controlling block of stock

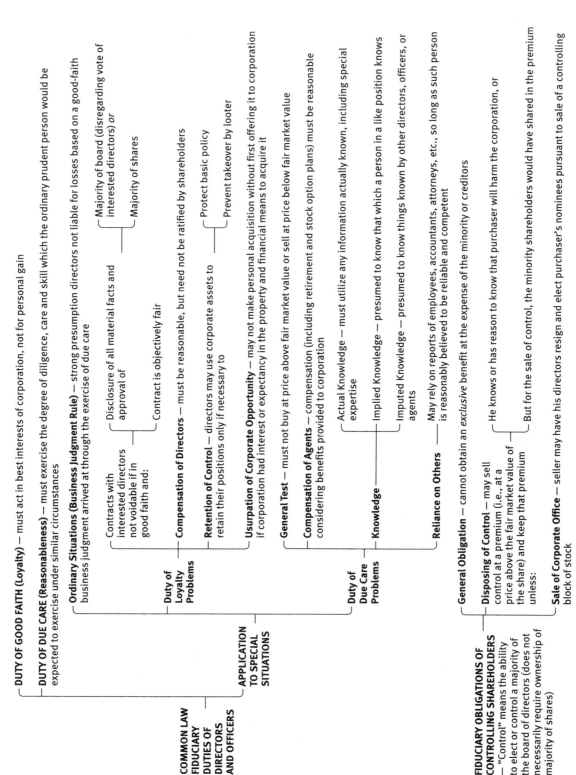

3b. INSIDER TRADING

Actions by Buyers from and Sellers to the insider

Special Facts Doctrine — officer or director with "special facts" has affirmative duty to disclose them or she is liable to person from whom she bought (privity required)

"FRAUD" UNDER SECTION 10(b) AND RULE 10b-5 — prohibited omissions and misstatement of material fact in connection with the purchase of sale of securities

Jurisdictional Requirement — use of an instrumentality of interstate commerce in connection with transaction

Possible Plaintiffs — SEC and any person buying or selling during period when insider was selling or buying

Possible Defendants — anyone with material, non-public information who trades in stock without disclosing this information

    Tippee Liability — non-insider who receives material, non-public information is liable if (a) inside information was factor in decision to buy or sell, *and* he knew or had reason to know that information was non-public

    Tippor Liability — person making a selective disclosure of material inside information is liable if (a) she is in a confidential relationship with the corporation, (b) she knew that information was material and non-public, *and* (c) she knew or had reason to know that tippee would trade on the basis of this information *(tippor need not be a purchaser or seller)*

Materiality — fact is material if there is a substantial likelihood that it would be considered important by a reasonable purchaser or seller

Scienter — must be at least reckless with regard to omission or misstatement

Reliance — must be proved in cases of misstatement, but presumed in omission cases upon proof of materiality

Remedies — rescission, injunction, or damages

(continued)

3b. INSIDER TRADING *(continued)*

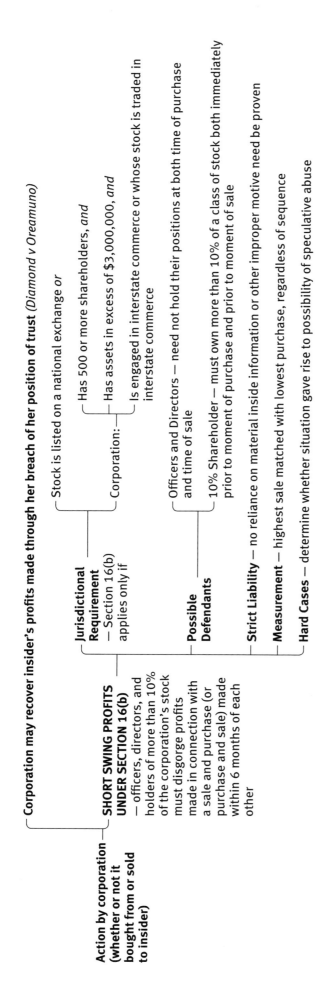

Corporation may recover insider's profits made through her breach of her position of trust *(Diamond v Oreamuno)*

Action by corporation (whether or not it bought from or sold to insider)

SHORT SWING PROFITS UNDER SECTION 16(b) — officers, directors, and holders of more than 10% of the corporation's stock must disgorge profits made in connection with a sale and purchase (or purchase and sale) made within 6 months of each other

Jurisdictional Requirement — Section 16(b) applies only if

Stock is listed on a national exchange *or*

Corporation:

Has 500 or more shareholders, *and*

Has assets in excess of $3,000,000, *and*

Is engaged in interstate commerce or whose stock is traded in interstate commerce

Possible Defendants

Officers and Directors — need not hold their positions at both time of purchase and time of sale

10% Shareholder — must own more than 10% of a class of stock both immediately prior to moment of purchase and prior to moment of sale

Strict Liability — no reliance on material inside information or other improper motive need be proven

Measurement — highest sale matched with lowest purchase, regardless of sequence

Hard Cases — determine whether situation gave rise to possibility of speculative abuse

4. SHAREHOLDER SUITS

DIRECT vs DERIVATIVE ACTIONS

Direct actions may be brought only to —
- Enforce inspection rights
- Enforce rights concerning proxies
- Require declaration of dividends
- Recover for fraud in relation to purchase or sale of stock
- Enforce appraisal remedy
- Object to dilution of voting rights (e.g., preemptive rights)
- Enforce a redemption agreement

Derivative Actions — other actions, which harm shareholders only indirectly, must be brought as derivative action

SPECIAL RULES FOR DERIVATIVE ACTIONS

STANDING
- **Contemporaneous Ownership Rule** — P must have been a shareholder at the time of the act complained of
  - Exception 1 — P obtained his stock through operation of law from a contemporaneous owner
  - Exception 2 — act complained of is a continuing wrong
- **Contemporary Ownership** — P must own stock at the time suit is brought and throughout the litigation

(continued)

4. SHAREHOLDER SUITS *(continued)*

DEMAND

On Directors — P required to make written demand on directors to bring suit unless demand would be futile

- Demand is futile if the directors are the defendants or the defendant controls the board

- A good-faith refusal by directors to bring suit bars a derivative action, including (perhaps) a refusal of a special litigation committee made up of disinterested directors

On Shareholders — traditionally, P must also make demand on shareholders, whose refusal to approve suit ratifies alleged wrong

- Exception 1 — demand excused when futile

- Exception 2 — demand excused when act complained of is fraudulent

- Exception 3 — demand may be excused if it would be unreasonably costly or time consuming

- Demand on shareholders not required at all in many states

BOND — The corporation may generally require a security bond for expenses unless P is a large shareholder (e.g., owns 5% of outstanding stock or $50,000 worth)

SPECIAL PROCEDURAL RULES

- **Corporation must be named as a defendant**

- **Jury trial possible if suit seeks money damages (as opposed to equitable relief)**

- **Action may not be discontinued without notice to other shareholders**

5. STOCK

TYPE OF STOCK
- COMMON — basic form of ownership
- PREFERRED — may have priority over common stock with regard to
  - DIVIDENDS
    - Cumulative Preferred — dividend preferences from past years must be paid before common stock receives any dividend
    - Non-Cumulative Preferred — past dividends which were not paid are lost forever
    - Participating Preferred — even after preference is paid, preferred shares still participate with common stock
  - LIQUIDATION
- CONVERTIBILITY — one form of stock may be exchanged for another form upon certain agreed conditions

ISSUANCE OF STOCK
- CONSIDERATION FOR SHARES — in most states, stock may be issued only for cash, tangible or intangible property, or services rendered
  - LIABILITY OF RECIPIENT
    - Statutory Obligation Theory — difference between value received and par is a corporate asset
    - Misrepresentation Theory — creditor who relied on balance sheet in extending credit may proceed directly against recipient
    - Defense — valuation of consideration received by directors is conclusive (if no fraud by recipient)
    - Does not escape liability by transferring watered stock to another
  - WATERED STOCK — stock with par value issued for consideration worth less than par
    - Liability of Transferee — no liability if purchased without knowledge that stock was watered
    - Liability of Directors — strictly liable for water (*NOTE:* even if par is received, directors breach duty of due care if stock is issued at below *fair market value*)
- PREEMPTIVE RIGHTS — shareholders right to maintain proportionate ownership of corporation when corporation issues new stock
  - Existence depends on stage statute and articles
  - Right of first refusal only — shareholder not required to buy, and corporation need not give special terms
  - Exceptions — (1) issuance is of a different class of stock, (2) shares are treasury stock, (3) shares are issued for consideration other than cash (services, debts cancelled, or property), or (4) part of price offering (unless long period has passed and consideration received is used for expansion)
- STOCK SUBSCRIPTIONS — agreement concerning purchase of stock in future
  - Subscriber's offer generally irrevocable for 3-6 months if corporation has not yet been formed unless subscription agreement provides otherwise or all subscribers consent
  - Corporation must treat all subscribers of a given class equally
  - Subscriber Defenses — (1) corporation never properly formed, (2) breach of express conditions (e.g., subscriptions received as to entire issuance), (3) fraud in the inducement, or (4) material change in corporate purpose or capital structure

TRANSFER OF SHARES
- MECHANICS — governed by UCC Article 8 (analogous to transference of negotiable instruments under UCC Article 3)
- RESTRICTIONS
  - Right of first refusal valid
  - MUST BE REASONABLE
    - Required sale by shareholder or purchase by corporation or other shareholders upon pre-agreed condition valid if agreement reasonable at time made
    - Requirement of director or shareholder approval is invalid in most states
  - NARROWLY CONSTRUED
  - TRANSFEREE NOT BOUND BY RESTRICTION UNLESS
    - Restriction appears or is referred to on stock certificate
    - Transferee had actual notice of restriction at time of acquisition

6. CORPORATE ACCOUNTING & CORPORATE DISTRIBUTIONS

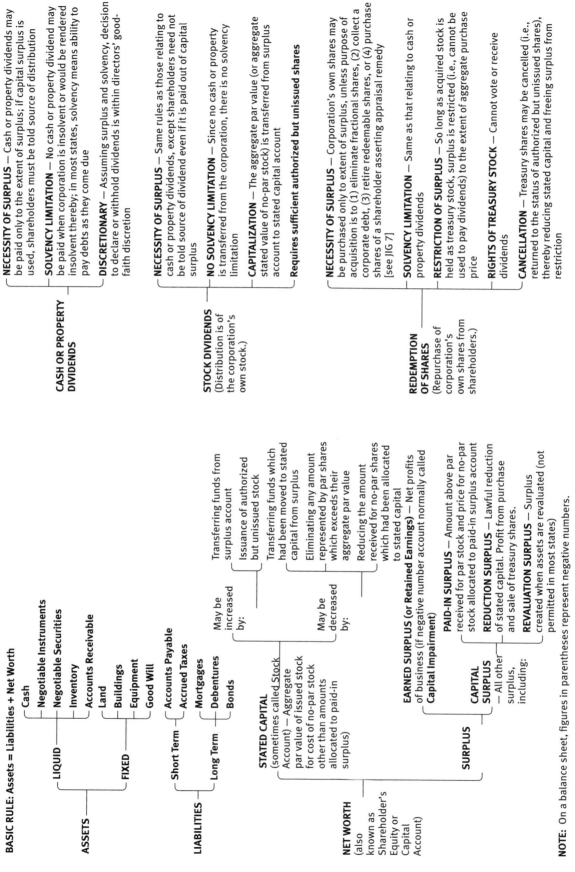

BASIC RULE: Assets = Liabilities + Net Worth

ASSETS

LIQUID
- Cash
- Negotiable Instruments
- Negotiable Securities
- Inventory
- Accounts Receivable

FIXED
- Land
- Buildings
- Equipment
- Good Will

LIABILITIES

Short Term
- Accounts Payable
- Accrued Taxes

Long Term
- Mortgages
- Debentures
- Bonds

NET WORTH (also known as Shareholder's Equity or Capital Account)

STATED CAPITAL (sometimes called Stock Account) — Aggregate par value of issued stock for cost of no-par stock other than amounts allocated to paid-in surplus)

SURPLUS — All other surplus, including:

May be increased by:
- Transferring funds from surplus account
- Issuance of authorized but unissued stock

May be decreased by:
- Transferring funds which had been moved to stated capital from surplus
- Eliminating any amount represented by par shares which exceeds their aggregate par value
- Reducing the amount received for no-par shares which had been allocated to stated capital

EARNED SURPLUS (or Retained Earnings) — Net profits of business (if negative number account normally called Capital Impairment)

CAPITAL SURPLUS

PAID-IN SURPLUS — Amount above par received for par stock and price for no-par stock allocated to paid-in surplus account

REDUCTION SURPLUS — Lawful reduction of stated capital. Profit from purchase and sale of treasury shares.

REVALUATION SURPLUS — Surplus created when assets are revaluated (not permitted in most states)

CASH OR PROPERTY DIVIDENDS

NECESSITY OF SURPLUS — Cash or property dividends may be paid only to the extent of surplus; if capital surplus is used, shareholders must be told source of distribution

SOLVENCY LIMITATION — No cash or property dividend may be paid when corporation is insolvent or would be rendered insolvent thereby; in most states, solvency means ability to pay debts as they come due

DISCRETIONARY — Assuming surplus and solvency, decision to declare or withhold dividends is within directors' good-faith discretion

STOCK DIVIDENDS (Distribution is of the corporation's own stock.)

NECESSITY OF SURPLUS — Same rules as those relating to cash or property dividends, except shareholders need not be told source of dividend even if it is paid out of capital surplus

NO SOLVENCY LIMITATION — Since no cash or property is transferred from the corporation, there is no solvency limitation

CAPITALIZATION — The aggregate par value (or aggregate stated value of no-par stock) is transferred from surplus account to stated capital account

Requires sufficient authorized but unissued shares

REDEMPTION OF SHARES (Repurchase of corporation's own shares from shareholders.)

NECESSITY OF SURPLUS — Corporation's own shares may be purchased only to extent of surplus, unless purpose of acquisition is to (1) eliminate fractional shares, (2) collect a corporate debt, (3) retire redeemable shares, or (4) purchase shares of a shareholder asserting appraisal remedy [see JIG 7]

SOLVENCY LIMITATION — Same as that relating to cash or property dividends

RESTRICTION OF SURPLUS — So long as acquired stock is held as treasury stock, surplus is restricted (i.e., cannot be used to pay dividends) to the extent of aggregate purchase price

RIGHTS OF TREASURY STOCK — Cannot vote or receive dividends

CANCELLATION — Treasury shares may be cancelled (i.e., returned to the status of authorized but unissued shares), thereby reducing stated capital and freeing surplus from restriction

NOTE: On a balance sheet, figures in parentheses represent negative numbers.

7. FUNDAMENTAL CHANGES (All these changes requiring filing with the Secretary of State)

AMENDMENTS TO ARTICLES — anything that might properly have been contained in original articles may be added by amendment

— **Shareholders** — by majority approval of the outstanding shares entitled to vote

— **Restated Articles** — board may integrate all amendments and original articles into a single document, without shareholder approval, if there is no further amendment

Shareholders must be given a summary of the proposed amendment or the changes to be made thereby with the notice of the meeting

— **Class approval** —
  — If any class is entitled to vote thereon as a class, the majority of each such class is required
  — Class approval also required, whether or not the class normally votes, if the amendment adversely affects the preferences or special rights of that class

MERGERS — acquisition of one corporation by another (A and B join with A surviving and B dissolving)

— **Directors of both corporations must approve**

— **Shareholder Approval** — a summary of the plan of merger must be presented to the shareholders with the notice of the meeting at which the vote is to be taken

  — **Acquired Corporation** — shareholders must approve by a majority vote of all shares entitled to vote

  — **Acquiring Corporation** — in some states, shareholders must approve only if merger (1) requires amendment to articles, (2) the number of shares they hold in the corporation will change, or (3) securities issued to shareholders of acquired corporation exceed 20 percent of common stock of surviving corporation outstanding immediately before merger

  — **Class voting may be required (see above, under Amendments)**

  — **Short-Form Merger** — a parent corporation may acquire its subsidiary without a vote of the subsidiary's shareholders if parent owns at least 90 percent of subsidiary's stock

— **Dissenting Shareholders** — may be entitled to appraisal rights (see below)

CONSOLIDATIONS — joining of two corporations with new corporation created (A and B join with C created and both A and B being dissolved)

— **Same rules as with Mergers (above), except that shareholders of *both* corporations must always approve**

(continued)

7. FUNDAMENTAL CHANGES (All these changes requiring filing with the Secretary of State) *(continued)*

SALES OF ALL OR SUBSTANTIALLY ALL ASSETS

- **Defined**
  - **Must deprive seller of ability to carry on business**
  - **Must not be in the ordinary course of business**
  - **Includes lease of assets, but not a mortgage**

- **Same rules as with Mergers (above), except that the shareholders of the acquiring corporations never have to approve**
  - **De Facto Merger Doctrine** — some cases have been treated purchase of assets as a merger when justice so required.

- **May be abandoned by the Directors notwithstanding shareholder approval**

APPRAISAL REMEDY (Right to Dissent) — dissenting shareholders may be able to require corporation to purchase their stock at its fair value on day before approval, disregarding the effect on the value caused by the proposal

- **Who May Dissent (in general)** — any shareholder entitled to vote on a merger, consolidation, or sale of assets and minority shareholders of a subsidiary acquired by short-form merger; some states also give right to shareholders whose special rights are adversely affected by amendment to articles

- **Procedural Requirements**
  - **Must give written notice of dissent to corporation prior to shareholder vote**
  - **Must not vote for the transaction**
  - **Must make written demand after the vote approving the transaction**
  - **May have to dissent as to all shares owned**

- **Limitations** — in some states, there is no right to appraisal
  - **The shares are publicly traded**
  - **In the case of a sale of assets, (1) when the net proceeds will be distributed to the shareholders in cash within 1 year, or (2) when sale is pursuant to court order**

DISSOLUTION

- **Typical Methods and Grounds**
  - **By incorporators or directors if business has not commenced and shares have not been issued**
  - **Naturally upon terms stated in the articles**
  - **By approval of all shareholders**
  - **By approval of directors and majority of shares entitled to vote**
  - **By Attorney General for (1) fraudulent organizations, or (2) repeated and willful fraudulent acts or acts in excess of authority**
  - **By Secretary of State for failure to file annual report, pay privilege fee, appoint a resident agent, or failure to notify the state of a change of the registered offices or agent**
  - **By the court for deadlock, oppression, or insolvency**

- **Winding Up** — upon dissolution, corporation must collect and liquidate its assets, pay its debts, and distribute the proceeds to shareholders

1. ELEMENTS OF CRIMES

ACT (ACTUS REUS) — law does not punish for thought alone; D must do some criminally cognizable act.

VOLITIONAL ACT — normally D must cause a criminally proscribed result by some *voluntary affirmative act*; look for indicia of lack of volition or control such as (1) *epilepsy*, (2) *automatism*, or (3) *hypnotism* (duress is *not* a volitional act defense).

OMISSION — if D has a *legal duty, failure to act is sufficient.*

- **STATUTE** — duty explicitly imposed by a statute (e.g., file tax returns).
- **CONTRACT** — duty imposed by agreement (e.g., lifeguard, nurse).
- **SPECIAL DEPENDENCY** — strong moral duty *plus* knowledge that person is *dependent and relying on D* (e.g., aged relative, young child, seamen–sea captain).
- **DETRIMENTAL UNDERTAKING** — if D commences to aid and leaves victim in worse position (some states make the mere undertaking a basis for duty even without detriment).
- **CAUSATION** — if D causes victim's plight, even without fault, some states require D to aid.

VICARIOUS LIABILITY — D may be responsible for act of another.

- **RESPONDEAT SUPERIOR** — acts of employees in strict liability regulatory crimes.
- **UNRESPONSIBLE AGENT** — acts of unresponsible agent (e.g., a child or insane person) caused by D.
- **ACCOMPLICE CONDUCT** — reasonably foreseeable acts of an accomplice.
- **CO-CONSPIRATOR CONDUCT** — acts of co-conspirators done to further the conspiratorial goal.

INTENT (MENS REA) — criminal law focuses on the *culpability* (e.g., blameworthiness) of D by examining his *state of mind with regard to the criminal consequence* (see Mens Rea JIG).

- **PURPOSEFUL** — if D does an act with the *conscious object of causing the criminal result.*
- **KNOWING** — if D does an act consciously aware of the fact that a criminal result is *practically certain.*
- **RECKLESS** — if D is consciously aware of the fact that his act creates a *substantial and unjustifiable risk that a criminal result will occur.*
- **NEGLIGENT** — if D *creates an unreasonable risk that a criminal result will occur.*
- **VOLUNTARY** — if D does a *volitional act which causes a criminal result* (i.e., strict liability).

(continued)

1. ELEMENTS OF CRIMES *(continued)*

CAUSATION — D's act must cause the particular result proscribed by the definition of the crime.

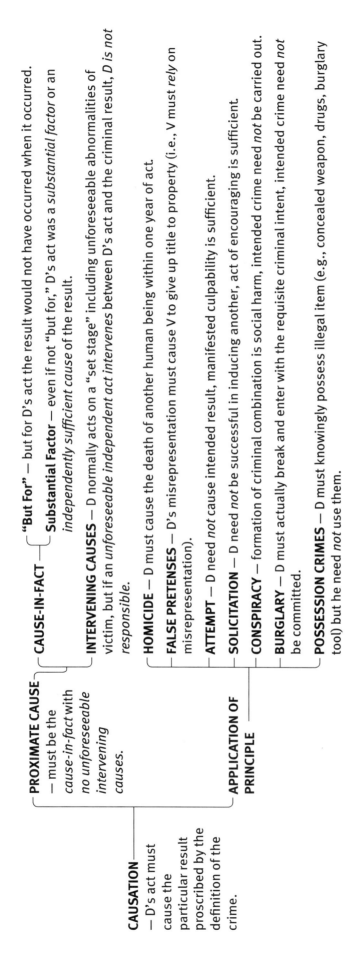

PROXIMATE CAUSE — must be the *cause-in-fact* with *no unforeseeable intervening causes.*

CAUSE-IN-FACT

- **"But For"** — but for D's act the result would not have occurred when it occurred.
- **Substantial Factor** — even if not "but for," D's act was a *substantial factor* or an *independently sufficient cause* of the result.

INTERVENING CAUSES — D normally acts on a "set stage" including unforeseeable abnormalities of victim, but if an *unforeseeable independent act intervenes* between D's act and the criminal result, *D is not responsible.*

APPLICATION OF PRINCIPLE

- **HOMICIDE** — D must cause the death of another human being within one year of act
- **FALSE PRETENSES** — D's misrepresentation must cause V to give up title to property (i.e., V must *rely* on misrepresentation).
- **ATTEMPT** — D need *not* cause intended result, manifested culpability is sufficient.
- **SOLICITATION** — D need *not* be successful in inducing another, act of encouraging is sufficient
- **CONSPIRACY** — formation of criminal combination is social harm, intended crime need *not* be carried out.
- **BURGLARY** — D must actually break and enter with the requisite criminal intent, intended crime need *not* be committed.
- **POSSESSION CRIMES** — D must knowingly possess illegal item (e.g., concealed weapon, drugs, burglary tool) but he need *not* use them.

2. MENS REA

ISSUE SPOTTING SEQUENCE

(1) What state of mind is required by the crime charged?

(2) What was D's state of mind with regard to the criminally proscribed consequence at the time he did the act causing that consequence?

(3) Are there any special facts negating D's culpability (i.e., any mens rea defenses)?

REQUIRED MENTAL STATE

SPECIFIC INTENT — *purpose or knowledge* that act will cause a particular criminal result.

INDICATIVE LANGUAGE

Intentional, Deliberate, Willful (Purposeful) — words requiring an act with the *conscious object* to cause a particular result (regardless of the likelihood of achieving result).

Knowingly, With Knowledge — requiring *conscious awareness* that conduct is *practically certain* to cause a particular result (regardless of D's desire to cause result).

THE BIG 7: BAM ACTS — (1) Burglary; (2) Assault — intent to batter or to frighten; (3) Murder *—intent-to-kill forms only*; (4) Attempt; (5) Conspiracy; (6) Theft; (7) Solicitation.

MEN'S REA DEFENSES — (1) *insanity*; (2) *diminished capacity*; (3) *intoxication* (voluntary or involuntary); (4) *mistake of fact* (even if unreasonable).

GENERAL INTENT — D must be at least *grossly and culpably negligent* with regard to causing the criminal result.

INDICATIVE LANGUAGE

Recklessly, Maliciously — requiring that D is *consciously aware* that his act creates a *substantial and unjustifiable risk* that a particular result will be caused.

Criminal Negligence — more than "mere negligence," requiring that D's conduct manifest a *gross and culpable departure from standards of reasonableness* with regard to a particular result (D need *not* be aware of risk). Normally, only used in homicide cases dealing with autos, guns, drugs, or risk of fire.

Statutory Construction — a statute proscribing conduct without specifying level of mens rea is normally *construed to require recklessness.*

THE LITTLE 4: BRIM — (1) Battery; (2) Rape; (3) Involuntary Manslaughter; (4) Murder — *other than intent-to-kill forms*.

MENS REA DEFENSES — (1) *insanity*; (2)*involuntary intoxication*; (3)*reasonable mistake of material fact.*

MORALITY CRIMES: CABS — (1) Contributing to delinquency of a minor; (2) Adultery; (3) Bigamy; (4) Statutory Rape.

STRICT LIABILITY — D may be convicted if his *voluntary act* caused the criminally proscribed result.

TRAFFIC, SAFETY, AND WELFARE REGULATIONS — where normal punishment is quasi-crime (e.g., fine or revocation of license), administrative necessity justifies liability without culpability.

ULTRAHAZARDOUS ACTIVITIES — persons dealing with firearms, explosives, food, alcohol and drugs held to maximum standard of care by imposition of strict liability.

MENS REA DEFENSES — none, strict liability requires only a voluntary act.

DETERMINING MENTAL STATE

PRESUMPTION — D is *presumed* to intend to cause the *natural and probable consequences* of his conduct.

EVIDENCE OF INTENT — look for direct statements by D or circumstantial evidence (such as motive) which tend to indicate D's state of mind with respect to the criminally proscribed consequences.

(continued)

KAPLAN PMBR

2. MENS REA *(continued)*

MENS REA DEFENSES

INSANITY

M'NAGHTEN TEST (majority rule) — D not criminally responsible if (1) *at the time of the offense* D was (2) *laboring under such a defect of reason from a disease of the mind* as (3) *not to know (a)the nature and quality of his act or, if he did know it, (b) he did not know that the act was wrong.*

IRRESISTIBLE IMPULSE (supplementary M'Naghten in many states) — D not criminally responsible if (1) *at the time of the offense,* D (2) *was unable to control his conduct* (3) *as a result of mental disease.*

ALI/MPC TEST — D not criminally responsible if (1) *at the time of the offense,* (2) *as a result of mental disease or defect,* she (3) *lacks substantial capacity to either (a) appreciate the criminality of her conduct, or (b) to conform her conduct to the requirements of the law.*

PROOF — insanity is an affirmative defense, but once D introduces evidence of insanity, burden of proof shifts to prosecutor to show D is not insane.

COMPETENCY — regardless of D's mental state at the time of the offense, an accused *cannot be tried* for a crime if (1) *at the time of trial,* she is (2) (a) *incapable of understanding the nature of the proceedings,* or (b) *of assisting in her defense in a rational or reasonable manner.*

DIMINISHED RESPONSIBILITY

MENTAL DEFICIENCY — about 12 states permit evidence of mental deficiency short of insanity to negate deliberation requirements of first degree murder; California allows mental illness to negate malice aforethought and reduce an intentional murder to voluntary manslaughter.

INTOXICATION — *involuntary intoxication* is a defense to any crime; it *may negate a required mental state* if D is so intoxicated that *he did not understand the criminal nature of his conduct; voluntary intoxication may* (1) *negate specific intent element of an offense if (2) before he formulates the criminal intent he* (3) *becomes so intoxicated that he lacked the capacity for culpability.*

INFANCY — children under 7 cannot crimes; 7–14, child presumed incapable of crime, but prosecution can rebut with evidence that child actually understood his conduct was wrong; over 14 children may be treated as adults (subject to state juvenile laws).

MISTAKE OF FACT

SPECIFIC INTENT CRIMES — any material mistake of fact (whether reasonable or unreasonable) negates specific intent.

GENERAL INTENT CRIMES — a reasonable mistake of material fact negates recklessness or negligence required by general intent crime.

MISTAKE OF LAW — generally no defense, but MPC allows defense if (1) D *reasonably relied upon official interpretation of a law which was later declared invalid;* (2) *without fault, D was not apprised of administrative rule;* (3) *if knowledge of legal status is an element of the offense; or* (4) *where statute requires an affirmative act.*

KAPLAN *pmbr*

3. ATTEMPTS

D is guilty of an attempt to commit a crime if: (1) with the *specific intent to cause a criminal result*, he (2) *does some legally sufficient act toward the commission of* the intended crime.

SPECIFIC INTENT — D must be either purposeful or knowing with regard to causing the result proscribed by the underlying crime; always look for specific intent defenses, especially intoxication and exculpating mistake. Remember, specific intent is required for all attempts, even if substantive crime is strict liability (e.g., attempted bigamy).

SUFFICIENT ACT — must be beyond mere preparation; a question of law for the judge.

LAST ACT — the *last act* required of D is always sufficient, even if subsequent acts of another are necessary (e.g., P puts poison in V's pills on nightstand).

UNEQUIVOCAL ACT — if D's act *unequivocally manifests criminal intent* it is sufficient (very often even the last act does not do this, however).

CORROBORATING ACT — best view focuses upon the significance of D's act in *demonstrating that D had the firm and present intent to commit the crime* (under this view the act must corroborate the existence of firm intent).

IMPOSSIBILITY

FACTUAL IMPOSSIBILITY — *if crime would have resulted had the facts been as D thought they were, impossibility is no defense*: (1) *inherently inadequate instrumentality* (D mistakes sugar for poison); (2) *error in time or place* (D attempts to "pick" an empty pocket, or kill a person already dead). Factual impossibility is based upon a mistake which does *not* negate culpability (i.e., D is worse than he appears).

STATUS OF GOODS — some courts hold that D cannot be guilty of an attempt to possess stolen property if property possessed is not in fact "stolen" (i.e., true owner consented to use of property to apprehend D). Under this view, a mistake as to the legal status of a thing provides a valid defense. Most courts and MPC treat this as factual impossibility (rather than legal impossibility) and deny the defense.

LEGAL IMPOSSIBILITY

INTENDED RESULT IS NOT ILLEGAL — if D believes an act is illegal but it is not, he cannot be guilty of an attempt simply by doing that act since the conduct actually intended is not regarded as socially harmful, thus, D must manifest a willingness to do an act actually proscribed by law.

DEFINITION OF CRIME EXCLUDES D — if, according to the definition of a crime, it is impossible for D to commit the substantive offense, there can be no attempt by D.

ABANDONMENT — crime of attempt is complete once a legally sufficient act has been committed, but some courts and MPC allow a defense if D (1) *voluntarily abandons the criminal act* (2) *prior to completion of the substantive crime* (3) *under circumstances manifesting a complete renunciation of criminal intent*. Look for extrinsic causes of withdrawal which are *not defenses* (e.g., fear of apprehension, selection of a different victim, etc.)

KAPLAN) pmbr

4. CONSPIRACY

(1) Agreement between (2) two or more persons (3) who have the specific intent (4) to either (a) commit a crime or (b) to engage in dishonest, fraudulent or immoral conduct injurious to public health or morals.

AGREEMENT
— there must be a *true agreement* to promote or facilitate a particular objective

AGREEMENT SUFFICIENT — at common law, the agreement itself is the only act required to complete the crime; federal and about half of states now require some *additional overt act* in furtherance of the conspiracy (although the act need not be illegal in itself and only one conspirator need do an act).

PROOF — agreement may be inferred from concert of action (look for mutual adoption of a common purpose).

FALSE AGREEMENT — secret police agent or other "false agreement" situations are not conspiracies — there must be true actual intent to carry out unlawful objective by at least two parties. (MPC is contra; party with true intent is still liable).

UNKNOWN CONSPIRATORS — D must agree with at least one other person but need *not* agree with (or even know identity of) all other members of the conspiracy.

SINGLE OR MULTIPLE CONSPIRACY — the agreement is the essence of conspiracy; thus, there is only one conspiracy even if agreement encompasses separate diverse criminal acts and even if agreement entails a continuous course of criminal conduct.

STATUS DEFENSE TO SUBSTANTIVE CRIME — if D conspires with B, it is no defense to either party that D may not be capable under the legal definition to commit underlying crime himself (e.g., a man cannot rape his own wife).

DIPLOMATIC IMMUNITY — that one party is immune from prosecution is no defense to other party.

DIMINISHED CAPACITY DEFENSES — if B, the only other conspirator, possesses a diminished capacity defense negating specific intent (e.g., intoxication, infancy, insanity), a few courts preclude conviction of D as well as B; better view including MPC permits convictions of D regardless of B's *personal mens rea defenses.*

TWO OR MORE PERSONS

ACQUITTAL ON MERITS — if B, the *only* other conspirator, is acquitted *on the merits* (i.e., not because of procedural or personal mens rea defenses), D may not be convicted.

HUSBAND-WIFE — today, D may conspire with a spouse (not so at old common law).

WHARTON'S RULE

Consent Crimes — if crime logically requires the voluntary participation of another (e.g., bribery, incest, adultery, gambling), there is no conspiracy unless agreement involves an *additional person not logically essential.*

Plurality Required by Substantive Crime — if substantive crime requires a number of participants (e.g., 5 or more conducting gambling operations), there can be no separate charge of conspiracy *unless* agreement involves persons who are not guilty of the substantive crime itself.

Model Penal Code — abandons Wharton's Rule.

4. CONSPIRACY *(continued)*

SPECIFIC INTENT — D must have the specific intent with regard to a criminal objective.

MENS REA DEFENSES APPLY — D may assert any mens rea defenses which negate specific intent.

PURPOSEFUL AGREEMENT — it is always sufficient that D enters the agreement with the conscious object of causing, promoting or facilitating a result which he knows to be criminal.

CORRUPT MOTIVE DOCTRINE — many states require that D actually had a *corrupt motive* (that he knew that intended conduct was illegal) except where the act is inherently wrong.

Mere Knowledge — normally not sufficient, but conviction is possible if: (1) goods supplied are *highly dangerous* (e.g., explosives), or *highly regulated* (e.g., drugs); (2) the crime is *very serious* (e.g., homicide, kidnapping); (3) there is *continuous involvement*, or (4) if D *affirmatively encouraged* use more of his goods when he had reason to know that the use was illegal.

Knowledge Plus Stake — D may be convicted if he *knows* that his goods or services are used for a criminal purpose *and* he has a *"stake" in the success of the criminal objective* (e.g., D charges an inflated price).

CONSPIRATORIAL OBJECTIVE

CRIME — it is a conspiracy to agree to commit any crime, including a misdemeanor.

PUBLICLY INJURIOUS ACT — it is a conspiracy to agree with another to do any act (even if lawful) which is injurious to public health or morals and is accomplished by dishonest, fraudulent, corrupt or immoral means (MPC and some states are *contra* limiting conspiracies to "crimes").

DEFENSES

ABANDONMENT — once a conspiracy has been formed, it is no defense that D subsequently withdrew, even if done prior to the completion of the underlying crime. (MPC and some states *contra*, but only if D: (1) completely renounces criminal purpose, *and* (2) makes substantial efforts to prevent the commission of the underlying crime.)

IMPOSSIBILITY — factual impossibility is not a defense though D may prevail if the conspiratorial objective is simply not illegal, regardless of D's contrary belief.

(continued)

4. CONSPIRACY *(continued)*

SEPARATE OFFENSE — conspiracy is a separate offense, distinct from the underlying crime (i.e., there is no merger).

VENUE — a criminal charge may be brought in any county where some act in furtherance was committed by any party, *or* where the agreement was made.

HEARSAY EVIDENCE — in a trial for conspiracy, otherwise inadmissable hearsay statements of co-conspirators are admissible against D if *made in furtherance of the conspiracy.*

SPECIAL CONSEQUENCES

VICARIOUS LIABILITY

General Rule — in addition to conspiracy and the substantive crime intended, D may be convicted of other crimes committed by members of conspiracy *in furtherance of conspiratorial goal* (it is no defense that D did not intend nor know of the acts.)

Chain Conspiracy — if D is part of a "chain" of known illegal acts (e.g., smuggling–wholesaling–retailing of drugs), he is liable for all crimes committed to further the conspiratorial goal (look for *"community of interest"*).

Wheel Conspiracy — if D conspires with B and B enters into similar separate and unrelated agreements for similar crimes with X and Y, B is the "hub" of a "wheel conspiracy;" if there is a *community of interest* so that D, X, and Y are interested in the success of each other's agreements with B, there is a "rim" connecting all the "spokes" in *one conspiracy* and all parties are liable for the criminal acts of the others. If there is no community of interest, there are 3 separate conspiracies and only B is liable for the acts of all others (as well as for 3 conspiracies).

ATTEMPTED CONSPIRACY (SOLICITATION) — one who attempts to induce, encourage or command another to commit a crime is guilty of solicitation; if the other person agrees there is conspiracy.

DURATION — vicarious liability lasts until the goal of the conspiracy is achieved (including *immediate escape*) or D withdraws by informing all co-conspirators. (In many states, D must make some substantial effort to prevent the crime.)

5a. CRIMINAL HOMICIDE ISSUES

Issue Spotting Sequence: (1) Is D responsible for an *act* causing the death? (2) Was D's act the *cause* of the death? (3) Was the act directed at *another* person? (4) Was the person *living* at the time of the act? (5) Did D possess a *criminal intent* with respect to the death? (6) Was there any *legal justification*?

ACT

Voluntary Affirmative Act — act is sufficient even if it is itself lawful and/or inherently non dangerous. If immediate killing act was involuntary due to epileptic seizure or sudden unconsciousness, look to see whether the last voluntary act done by D was done with awareness of possibility of loss of control.

Omission — death caused by D's failure to do an act he had a *legal duty* to do as the result of: (1) special statute, (2) contractual delegation, (3) special relationship of dependency, (4) voluntary undertaking (if abandonment puts victim in worse position) or (5) D's innocent act imperils victim.

Vicarious Liability — D is responsible for homicidal acts of: (1) unresponsible agents put into motion by D, (2) accomplices—if act was reasonably foreseeable, and (3) co-conspirators—if act was done in furtherance of the conspiratorial goal (whether it was foreseeable or not).

CAUSE

Cause-in-fact

But For — D's act was a necessary condition of result; "but for" the act, the victim would have lived longer.

Independently Sufficient — even if not the "but for" cause, D's act was sufficient in itself to produce result.

Substantial Factor — even if not either the "but for" cause or an independently sufficient cause, D's act was at least a substantial factor in producing result.

Outside Time Limit — at common law, the victim must die within a year and a day of the injury inflicted by D. Modern states extend time up to 3 years.

Proximate Cause

Pre-existing Conditions — D "takes his victim as he finds him" and acts on a "set stage," therefore, even unknown and unforeseeable pre-existing conditions which contribute to V's death do *not* intervene to break the chain of causations. Though D is criminally responsible for the direct results of his conduct from a causation stand point, unusually unforeseeable conditions may create a mens rea defense.

Intervening Causes — a separate event or act which occurs between D's cause-in-fact conduct and the death will *supercede* D's act and break the chain of causation if the intervening act or event was: (1) *Independently sufficient* to cause the death, (2) *unforeseeable*, and (3) an *independent* act of god or another person not directly and logically flowing from D's act. (Some courts will also relieve D of responsibility if the intervening force was *dependent*). Failure of intervening rescue does *not* break the chain of causation.

(continued)

5a. CRIMINAL HOMICIDE ISSUES *(continued)*

DEATH OF ANOTHER — suicidal acts and attempts are not sufficient for homicide though many states separately punish attempted suicides especially if they endanger or injure innocent persons.

LIVING PERSON

Unborn Infants — a victim has to be "born alive" and separated from its mother before homicide responsibility can arise. Some courts hold that a "viable" unborn fetus is a person for homicide purposes if it was sufficiently developed to be capable of living independently from its mother. State has right to declare a fetus "alive" after the first trimester of pregnancy. *Roe v Wade.*

Comatose Victims — death occurs at the moment all bodily functions permanently cease, and not before. Because of life sustaining equipment that can support biological life and minimal body functions long after irreparable deterioration of the brain, the notion of "brain death" is a possible alternative.

CRIMINAL INTENT — homicide crimes are "graded" in terms of the culpability of D with respect to the death (See Flowchart 5A) but the following mental states are sufficient for some form of criminal homicide.

Specific Intent to Kill — D has the specific intent to kill if he is either *knowing* or *purposeful* with regard to the death. This includes willful, deliberate, premeditated and deliberate killings. Unless justified, all intentional killings are either murder or voluntary manslaughter. Intent to kill is an express form of malice aforethought.

Unintentional Killings — D can be guilty of criminal homicide even if there was no intent to kill at the time of the death-causing act. Unintentional killings may either be murder or manslaughter but intent is criminal if D: (1) *intends to cause great bodily harm, a forcible felony or resist a known lawful arrest,* (sufficient states for implied malice aforethought and, therefore, murder), (2) was *reckless* with regard to the death (wanton reckless disregard for human life is an extreme form sufficient for murder), (3) was *criminally negligent* with regard to the death, or (4) *intends to commit a malum in se unlawful act* (or inherently dangerous crime) not amounting to a forcible felony.

5a. CRIMINAL HOMICIDE ISSUES *(continued)*

LEGAL JUSTIFICATION
(See Flowchart 7)

Self Defense — at the time of the act D (1) *reasonably believed* (2) that the *amount of force used was necessary* to protect himself from (3) *imminent* (4) *great bodily harm or death*. D may not be aggressor and, in minority of states, he must retreat before using deadly force if he knows he can do so with complete safety (except in his own home).

Defense of Other — D's act was (1) done *in defense of another person* and (2) the *person defended had a legal right to use the same amount of force used by D*. D "stands in the shoes" of the person defended and his conduct is judged in terms of actual facts. MPC, N.Y., and modern view permit defense if D reasonably believed that person defended would have been legally justified in using the force employed by D. Some states require person defended to be a close relative.

Prevention of Crime — D's act was intended to (1) *prevent commission of a forcible felony* (e.g., burglary, arson, robbery, rape, kidnapping, felonius assault) which (2) was *actually being committed* and (3) the *force used was reasonably believed necessary*. MPC, N.Y., and modern view judge D in terms of his reasonable belief about the commission of the felony, not the actual facts.

Apprehension of Dangerous Felon — D's act was (1) *done to effectuate an arrest or prevent escape* of a person who (2) *actually* (3) had *committed a forcible felony*, (4) the *force used reasonably appeared to be necessary*, and (5) the *act did not unreasonably endanger innocent bystanders*. If D is a peace officer his conduct will be judged in terms of his reasonable belief as to the commission of the underlying felony, not by the actual facts.

Necessity — D's act was (1) *done to prevent imminent loss of life* (2) under circumstances where *according to ordinary standards of intelligence and morality* (3) the *harm sought to be avoided outweighed the harm caused by the act.*

Defenses not available — deadly force is *not* justified on a theory of *duress, entrapment, defense of property* (though if victim was committing a burglary or robbery prevention of a forcible felony justifies a killing); or *consent* ("mercy killing" or euthanasia is not a recognized defense but it can mitigate sentencing).

5b. HOMICIDE CRIMES

MURDER — Unlawful killing with malice aforethought, no degrees of murder at common law.

Intent to Kill — Includes both *purposeful* (conscious object) and *knowing* (practically certain) killings. Specific intent defenses available to negate mens rea. Under modern statutes, if intent to kill is supplemented by *deliberation* and *premeditation* (mental states revealing a relatively calm, "cold-blooded," reflective killing as opposed to a sudden, impulsive or spontaneous killing). If victim does not die, D is guilty of attempted murder.

Unintentional Killing — Wanton Reckless Disregard for Life — Unintended killing resulting from an act done with a *conscious and knowing* disregard of a *plain and strong likelihood* that an *unjustified death or serious injury will result*. Any facts which negate conscious awareness of the risk may prevent mens rea (but voluntary intoxication may not negate recklessness). More than "mere recklessness;" act must reveal a wanton depraved indifference to human life. If victim does not die, no attempted murder since no specific intent to kill.

Unintentional Killing — Intent to Cause Great Bodily Harm (GBH) — Unintended killing resulting from an act done with the purpose or knowledge that it cause *serious protracted injury* or create a *substantial risk of death* (very similar to recklessness). Includes any intentional wounding with a gun or knife, breaking of bones, clubbing, poisoning or an act designed to produce unconsciousness by drugs or violence. Intent to do GBH may be negated by mistake, extreme intoxication, and in minority, by diminished mental capacity. If victim does not die, no attempted murder. Under modern statutes unintended death resulting from *intentional use of poison or explosives, torture,* or *ambush* (lying in wait) is first degree.

Unintentional Killing — Intent to Resist Known Lawful Arrest — Unintended killing resulting from act done in resistance of a *known lawful arrest*. D must actually know that the arrest is under lawful authority and mens rea defenses may negate that knowledge. If victim does not die, no attempted murder.

Unintentional Killing — Intent to Commit a Felony — Unintended killing proximately caused by and during the commission of a felony or an attempted felony. Wide state variations as to the *nature of the underlying felony* (most limit to forcible felonies — burglary, arson, robbery, rape, kidnapping), the *degree of offense* (usually first degree), and *special limitations* (usually as to the status of the killer or victim). *No attempted murder if victim does not die.*

Special Limitations — modern view permits felony murder (FM) only if D or a criminal accomplice directly kills the victim and where victim is an innocent person (not an accomplice)

Underlying Felony Must be Proved — any defense to the underlying felony (e.g., claim of right to a burglary or robbery) absolves D of FM responsibility.

Perpetration — felony includes period from attempt (i.e., act beyond preparation) through immediate flight until final rest.

5b. HOMICIDE CRIMES *(continued)*

VOLUNTARY MANSLAUGHTER
An intentional murder "mitigated" by facts negating malice aforethought.

Intentional Killing — Provocation — Intentional killing done in the *heat of passion caused by legally sufficient provocation* (actual or threatened battery or perceived infidelity — *not mere words*). Provocation must be such that it might render a reasonable ordinary person to lose self control and act rashly. "Cooling off" period between provocation and killing act destroys defense. Normal range of physical and temperamental defects are *not* taken into account but extreme disabilities of a permanent nature *may* be considered by a liberal court. Modern trend is to liberalize types of legally sufficient provocation and focus on culpability; MPC allows any "extreme emotional disturbance" regardless of cause. If victim does not die, some courts hold D for *attempted voluntary manslaughter*; others only for felonious assault.

Intentional Killing — Mistaken Justification — Intentional killing done with an *actual* but *unreasonable or erroneous* belief that the act was legally justified. Includes use of excessive force, unreasonable belief that harm was imminent, error as to the rights of a person being defended, etc. — called *imperfect self defense*. If victim does not die, some convict of attempted voluntary manslaughter; others felonious assault.

Intentional Killing — Diminished Capacity — While most states allow evidence of mental defect short of insanity and extreme intoxication to negate the "premeditation" aspect (reducing a charge to second degree murder), a small minority go further and permit a showing of diminished mental capacity to *negate malice aforethought* and reduce the charge to voluntary manslaughter. Diminished capacity applies only to homicide charges.

(continued)

5b. HOMICIDE CRIMES (continued)

INVOLUNTARY MANSLAUGHTER
An unintentional unlawful killing without malice aforethought.

Unintentional Killing — Ordinary Recklessness — Unintended killing resulting from an act done with a *conscious disregard* for a *substantial* and *unjustifiable* risk of *death or serious injury* but one that does *not* demonstrate a wanton depraved indifference to human life. The distinction between ordinary recklessness resulting in involuntary manslaughter and depraved recklessness resulting in murder is merely a question of degree to be determined as an issue of fact.

Unintentional Killing — Gross and Culpable Negligence — Unintended killing resulting from a negligent act which reveals a wanton disregard of the risk of death or serious injury. More than ordinary negligence, it must be *gross* and *culpable* but it is *not* required that the prosecutor prove that D was consciously aware of the risk (compare to recklessness). Normally deals with mishandling of an *inherently dangerous instrumentality* (e.g., guns, explosives, automobiles), *product* (e.g., food and drugs) or *situation* (e.g., risk of fire in a public place).

Unintentional Killing — Unlawful Act Rule — Unintended killing proximately caused by and during the commission or attempted commission of a *malum in se* (i.e., wrong in itself) misdemeanor or felony (*if* jurisdiction limits FM rule to forcible felonies). Sometimes called the misdemeanor-manslaughter rule. Many states apply rule only to *inherently dangerous crimes* or *non-dangerous crimes committed in an unusual and inherently dangerous manner.* Look for this possibility whenever FM fails.

Unintentional Killing — Provocation and Mistaken Justification — Unintended killing resulting from an *act only intended to wound or frighten* done in the heat of passion with *legally sufficient provocation* or in *an honest but erroneous belief that the force used was legally justified,* (compare to voluntary manslaughter where the intent was to kill).

6. COMMON LAW BURGLARY

(1) Trespassory (2) breaking and (3) entering (4) a dwelling (5) in the nighttime (6) with specific intent to: (a) commit a larceny or (b) any felony (7) therein.

TRESPASSORY — entry must be without consent, but entry gained by misrepresentation of identity or other trick is trespassory.

BREAKING — D must create or enlarge the opening for his entry; includes opening an unlocked door or raising a partially open window, but D need not actually "break." In many states, unlawful "remaining" in a store after closing is a constructive breaking, though common law requires that the breaking must be done to gain entry, not to exit. Some states abandon the breaking requirement entirely.

ENTERING — D must physically intrude victim's property. ⌐

D'S BODY — any portion of D's body is sufficient.

INSTRUMENT — any tool or hook invading the property is sufficient if it is used to achieve the criminal purpose (as opposed to using it to merely gain entry).

INCLUDES CURTILAGE — structures immediately surrounding the dwelling (e.g., enclosed in the area of the "yard") and physically connected buildings.

INCLUDES BOATS AND TRAILERS WHERE PEOPLE SLEEP

MODERN STATUTES EXTEND TO ALL "ENCLOSED STRUCTURES" ABANDONING THE DWELLING REQUIREMENT

DWELLING — structure must be a place where one *normally* sleeps (though it need not be occupied at the time of entry).

NIGHTTIME — entry must occur 30 minutes before sunset or after sunrise. This requirement is *abandoned under modern "breaking and entering" statutes.*

SPECIFIC INTENT

Intent to Commit Any Larceny is Sufficient (even if petty larceny)

LARCENY — **Be Sure all Elements of Larceny are Specifically Intended:** (1) trespassory taking, (2) carrying away, (3) personal property, (4) known to be owned by another, (5) intent to permanently deprive. The claim of right defense is particularly likely to arise, if it does, there is no burglary.

ANY FELONY — intent to commit *any* felony is sufficient, but look for defenses to the underlying felony.

THEREIN — D must intend to commit the crime *in the dwelling* (or enclosed structure); it is not sufficient that D broke and entered only to get to another place.

7. JUSTIFICATION FOR THE USE OF FORCE

SELF-DEFENSE
— if D has a (1) *reasonable fear* of (2) *imminent* (3) *bodily harm* he may use (4) that amount of force which is *reasonably necessary* to prevent the harm (5) unless D is an *aggressor*.

REASONABLE FEAR — D must *actually* and *reasonably* believe that V is threatening imminent bodily harm (belief need not be correct).

IMMINENT HARM — *D must believe harm is imminent* although D may seize last reasonable opportunity to defend himself if V attempts to deprive him of the capacity for self-defense (as where V attempts to tie D up and torture him later). Note: If threat of harm is past, D has no right of self-defense.

BODILY HARM — "self defense" is not available to prevent or respond to insults regardless of how offensive or vile, *use of force justified only to prevent a reasonably anticipated battery.*

NECESSARY FORCE
— *short of deadly force*, D may use that amount of force that is *reasonably necessary to prevent the threatened harm;* if D uses *excessive force,* he becomes an aggressor and loses the right of self-defense.

DEADLY FORCE — (1) *force intended to cause death or* (2) *force creating a substantial likelihood of causing great bodily harm* (including death).

RECIPROCITY — D may only use deadly force to respond to deadly force.

RETREAT RULE (minority) — D may not use deadly force if he *actually knew he could have prevented the harm by retreating.*

D must subjectively believe that he could retreat in complete safety.

D need not retreat from his own home (many states include any place of nightly repose and some include offices and automobile).

AGGRESSOR LIMITATION

AGGRESSOR — D is an aggressor if (1) *he strikes the first blow* or (2) *commits a crime against V.*

REGAINING RIGHTS OF SELF-DEFENSE — aggressor regains the right to use force in self-defense if (1) *he abandons aggression completely and V actually perceives the abandonment,* or (2) *V uses excessive force.*

DEFENSE AGAINST UNLAWFUL ARREST — D may use reasonable, non-deadly force to prevent an unlawful arrest or unlawful attachment of her property, but she acts at her own risk; the arrest or attachment must, in fact, be unlawful or the defense is denied. (Modern view prevents all use of force to resist any arrest, even if unlawful.)

7. JUSTIFICATION FOR THE USE OF FORCE *(continued)*

DEFENSE OF OTHERS — in defending another person (V) from imminent injury, D is justified in using only the amount of force which V could use in his own defense; D stands in the shoes of V and if V was, in fact, the aggressor, the force used by D is not privileged. (MPC and modern trend allow D's conduct to be measured by the reasonable person standard — if D reasonably believed the force used was justified, the defense is valid.)

DEFENSE OF PROPERTY — modern day *non-deadly* force may be used to prevent theft, destruction or trespass of property. If deadly force was used, look to see whether it could be justified as *self defense* (e.g., as where D shot an armed robber) or *to prevent a dangerous forcible felony* (e.g., as where D shot a burglar intruding into his home).

LAW ENFORCEMENT DEFENSES — police officers and private citizens may use force in preventing crimes and effectuating an arrest. Normally, courts are more liberal in allowing force to *prevent* a crime (especially a felony) than in an after-the-crime arrest.

POLICE — may use amount of force, *including deadly force, which reasonably appears necessary* as long as force is *not disproportionate* to the offense involved or the resistance offered (Some states limit use of deadly force to prevent commission of a dangerous forcible felony or apprehension of a dangerous fleeing felon.)

CITIZEN — may use the same amount of force as police officer except *D acts at his own risk*; defense is denied if D is mistaken about the commission of the crime. (MPC and modern trend test D's conduct by reasonable person standard.)

NECESSITY — force, including deadly force, is justified to avoid an (1) imminent public or private injury, (2) resulting from natural physical forces, (3) which injury is about to occur through no fault of the actor and which is (4) of such gravity that (5) according to ordinary standards of intelligence and morality (6) the desirability of avoiding the injury clearly outweighs the state's interest in preventing the proscribed conduct.

8. CRIMINAL LAW

ACQUISITION BY STEALTH, FORCE, OR THREAT

LARCENY — (1) trespassory (2) taking and (3) carrying away of (4) personal property (5) known to be another's with (6) the intent to permanently deprive.

- **TRESPASSORY** — taking by stealth or force.
- **TAKING OF POSSESSION (caption)** — D must take possession and acquire dominion and control; there can be no larceny if D already has lawful possession.
- **CARRYING AWAY (asportation)** — larceny complete when D carries the property away from the point of taking; slight movement is sufficient.
- **PERSONAL PROPERTY** — D must take tangible personal property at common law, but most states have special statutes for theft of services and other intangibles.
- **OF ANOTHER** — D must specifically know the property is owned by another; any bona fide claim of right is a complete defense. Also look for mens rea defenses of mistake or intoxication.
- **INTENT TO PERMANENTLY DEPRIVE** — D must intend to *permanently* deprive the owner of the property *at the time of the taking*; no larceny if D intends to restore the identical property taken, but intent is sufficient if D: (1) intends to pay a cash equivalent at a later time, (2) intends to return only if a reward is paid, or (3) recklessly exposes property to loss.

ROBBERY — (1) larceny (be sure all elements are present) (2) from a person (3) accomplished by force or putting in fear (i.e., threat). Includes threat to person, his family, or his property.

- **FROM A PERSON** — taking from the "presence" of a person is sufficient if force or threat was needed to sever the property from the person's control.
- **FORCE OR THREAT** — must precede or accompany the taking. *Armed robbery* is an aggravated form where D uses a weapon or an article designed to look like a weapon.

EXTORTION — statutory extension of common law robbery consisting of (1) the use of malicious threats with the (2) specific intent to (3) compel a person to either (a) pay money, or (b) do or refrain from doing any act against his will (commonly referred to as "blackmail").

- **INJURY** — includes threats to injure V or his family or to injure V's property.
- **ACCUSATION** — includes threats to charge or prosecute V with a crime (whether or not V actually committed the crime) if used to cause V to do an act or pay money; claim of right is no defense.
- **DISGRACE** — includes threats to expose V to disgrace or extreme humiliation.
- **NEED NOT BE IMMEDIATE** — unlike robbery, the threat need not relate to an immediate harm.

8. CRIMINAL LAW *(continued)*

ACQUISITION BY FRAUD OR TRICK

OBTAINING PROPERTY BY FALSE PRETENSES — (1) *acquisition of title* (not mere possession) of (2) personal property (3) by means of a representation of fact (*not* a promise of future performance) (4) known by D to be false (5) at the time of acquisition.

TITLE — the owner must intend to convey permanent unfettered possession (i.e., title) to D in a *sale* or *trade* transaction.

REPRESENTATION — unlike larceny by trick, it is *not* sufficient that D makes a false promise; there must be misrepresentation of a present or past *fact* or there is no crime.

SCIENTER — D must know of the falsity of the representation at the time of acquisition.

RELIANCE — owner must actually rely on D's misrepresentation.

LARCENY BY TRICK — (1) taking of possession (not title) of (2) personal property (3) known to be owned by another (4) with the intent to permanently deprive (5) where such taking is accomplished by means of a representation or promise (6) known by D to be false (7) at the time of the taking.

POSSESSION — the owner must intend to convey only temporary possession to D in a *rental, loan,* or *bailment* transaction.

REPRESENTATION — includes misrepresentation of past or present facts *and* a false promise to return the property.

SCIENTER — D must actually know the representation or promise was false at the time of the taking.

RELIANCE — owner must actually rely on D's misrepresentation or D is only liable for attempt

CONVERSION

LARCENY BY CONVERSION — same as larceny by trick except that there is *no false representation;* the intent to permanently convert the property for D's own exclusive use must be formed *after* the lawful acquisition of possession in a rental, loan, or bailment situation.

CONVERSION — D need only apply the property to a *personal use* to be guilty, regardless of the intent to restore or even the actual restoration of the property.

PROPERTY — by some statutes includes title to real property.

EMBEZZLEMENT — a variation of larceny by conversion developed to deal with (1) the improper use (i.e., conversion) of (2) property (3) entrusted to D's custody; there is no need for the intent to permanently deprive and no need for a misrepresentation.

ENTRUSTMENT — D must have acquired custody of the property as a result of a special fiduciary relationship (e.g., trustee, agent, employee).

1. OVERVIEW

EXCLUSIONARY RULE — to deter unconstitutional police conduct, evidence will be excluded from D's trial

SEARCH AND SEIZURE — evidence resulting from an *unreasonable invasion* of D's *reasonable expectations* of privacy (including arrests and detentions) in the absence of a properly issued or executed warrant or conditions justifying the invasion without a warrant.

INTERROGATIONS — statements as well as confessions which were (1) *coerced*, (2) elicited during a *custodial interrogation* in the absence of warnings or waiver, (3) made *after arraignment* in the absence of D's lawyer, or (4) made during an *unreasonable delay* between arrest and arraignment.

IDENTIFICATIONS — evidence of a pretrial identification (or courtroom identification derived directly therefrom) made under circumstances where there was unnecessary suggestion which created a substantial likelihood of irreparable misidentification.

RIGHT TO COUNSEL — D has right to the assistance of *effective counsel* at all *critical stages* of a *criminal proceeding* including (1) custodial interrogations, and (2) arraignments if plea made, (3) preliminary hearings, (4) post indictment line-ups, (5) trials where *imprisonment is actually imposed*, (6) sentencing and probation proceedings and (7) appeals as a matter of right. Counsel must at least be "reasonably competent" under modern trend, but D is not entitled to appointed counsel of choice (i.e., no meaningful relationship required).

RELIABILITY AND FAIRNESS SAFEGUARDS — to assure a fair and accurate disposition of D

DUE PROCESS (FAIR TRIAL) — D is entitled to a trial free of error, influences or pressures which unjustifiably tend to affect the outcome (such as, (1) prejudicial pretrial *publicity*, (2) judicial or juror *bias*, (3) *intimidation*, (4) *improper comment*, (5) *failure of prosecutor to correct false testimony or disclose exculpatory evidence*). Statute requiring loiterers to provide "credible and reliable" identification violates due process. Where D exercises a statutory right to appeal misdemeanor convictions, a subsequent prosecution for a felony arising from the same facts violates due process because of an unrebutted presumption of prosecutorial vindictiveness.

BURDEN OF PROOF — prosecutor must prove all elements of the offense "beyond a reasonable doubt." Any presumption operating in a criminal case must be based upon reasonable inference and may not shift burden on each element to D. State may impose burden of proof on D with respect to certain *affirmative defenses* or *mitigating facts* (e.g., provocation) but may not instruct jury to presume intent from the facts.

CONFRONTATION AND PROCESS — D must have opportunity to compel attendance of witnesses in his defense and to cross-examine prosecution witnesses (although hearsay is permitted if qualified under reasonable rules of evidence).

1. OVERVIEW (continued)

INDIVIDUAL RIGHTS AND DIGNITY SAFEGUARDS — to protect D from arbitrary and unreasonable government conduct

JURY TRIAL — (1) D has right to an impartial (though not an ethnically balanced) jury *in all trials where imprisonment of 6 months or more is possible*; (2) a jury of 6 is sufficient, (3) a unanimous verdict is *not* constitutionally required; (4) peremptory challenges may be made even if racially motivated.

DOUBLE JEOPARDY — D may not be tried twice for the *same offense* unless the first trial ended in a *legally necessary mistrial* or the result was *reversed on D's appeal based on an error of law* (not sufficiency of evidence). Acquittal of criminal charges does not preclude a civil forfeiture of firearms. Collateral estoppel is a separate doctrine which precludes trial if D already acquitted of crime based on same facts.

RIGHT AGAINST SELF-INCRIMINATION — D may not be (1) required to testify in his own trial, or (2) if testifying in any case (civil or criminal), he may not be compelled to answer a question unless D has waived the right or has been granted proper "use immunity"; statutes which impose unreasonable requirements of disclosure violate this right; right applies only to *testimonial communications*; D entitled to a "no inference of guilt" instruction if D refuses to testify. D must produce business records under subpoena.

EQUAL PROTECTION — indigent D must be provided with: (1) *counsel* at all critical stages and on appeals permitted as a matter of right, (2) *free transcripts* (if required to perfect appeal), and (3) *possibly experts or investigators* necessary to an effective defense.

SPEEDY TRIAL — once D has been *formally charged*, he must be given a speedy trial; no absolute standard but courts consider (1) length of delay, (2) reason for delay, (3) whether D demanded early trial or caused delay, and (4) whether delay was prejudicial to a fair trial.

NOTICE OF CHARGES — D must be apprised of all elements of the offense in an indictment or information.

CRUEL AND UNUSUAL PUNISHMENT — D may not be punished for illness or status and penalty must be proportionate to crime (e.g., life sentence for writing a bad check is improper); death penalty not *per se* invalid but must be administered so as to consider the individual circumstances of D's crime; an accomplice who did not kill, attempt to kill, intend to kill or intend to use deadly force cannot be sentenced to death.

SENTENCING — D entitled to counsel but not to an adversary proceeding with cross-examination.

GUILTY PLEAS — valid if judge informs D of all rights and consequences (even without counsel) and determines that plea was voluntary and intelligently made (even if D asserts his innocence to the charge at the time of the plea).

JUVENILE PROCEEDINGS — D has right to (1) counsel, (2) confrontation, (3) notice of charges, (4) silence, and (5) proof beyond reasonable doubt; he has *no right* to (1) bail, (2) public trial, (3) jury trial, (4) indictment (applicability of exclusionary rule undecided).

RIGHT TO BAIL — a suspect awaiting trial has a constitutional right to be released on reasonable bail unless charged with a capital offense *and* the proof of guilt is evident.

2. EXCLUSIONARY RULE

PROCEDURAL ASPECTS — a (1) *timely motion to suppress* must be made by one with (2) *standing* (i.e., a reasonable expectation of privacy was invaded) and all (3) *fruits derived from the illegal conduct* (unless taint is dissipated by *independent source, inevitable discovery or attenuation*) where (4) *conduct was by a government agent* (i.e., *state action*) and (5) the evidence is *offered to prove guilt* of D (*not* for grand jury, impeachment, sentencing, etc.)

SEARCHES AND SEIZURES (S&S)

THRESHOLD QUESTION — Fourth Amendment requirements only apply if government invades a *reasonable expectation of privacy*; limitations do *not* apply to (1) *voluntary disclosures to indiscreet confidants*, (2) *bank records*, (3) *abandoned property*, (4) *pen registers*, (5) *voice exemplars*, (6) *"plain view" observations* (from a lawful vantage point), or (7) searches conducted with consent, (8) *"open fields"*, (9) *garbage left out for collection*, or (10) *dog sniffs of persons, luggage and the exterior of vehicles.*

WARRANT — S&S authorized by a warrant is valid if: (1) issued by *neutral magistrate*, (2) from facts under *oath*, (3) sufficient to allow *independent judgment* of the existence of (4) *probable cause* and the warrant (5) *specifically limits the intrusion* and is (6) *reasonably executed*. Searches made pursuant to reasonable *good faith* reliance on a defective warrant are valid

NO WARRANT — warrantless S&S is reasonable if: (1) officer has *probable cause* and (a) evidence could be *lost or destroyed by delay*, (i.e. exigent circumstances), (b) police are in *"hot pursuit"* of a felon or (c) suspected evidence is in an *automobile on the open highway* or an easily accessible public parking lot or (d) valid *consent* has been given; (2) the search is made *incident to a lawful inventory, stop or arrest*, or (3) occurs at or near an *international border*, or (4) the item is seized under the *"plain view"* doctrine.

ARRESTS — proper if authorized by *valid warrant* (see above) or without a warrant if it is a mere "stop" (i.e., temporary detention) based on *reasonable suspicion of criminality* or a "full blown arrest" based on *probable cause that suspect committed a felony*. An arrest takes place where a person detained reasonably believes he is not free to leave.

STATEMENTS AND CONFESSIONS — inadmissible if it was: (1) *involuntary*, (2) taken in violation of *Miranda* rule, (3) was taken after *formal charge in counsel's absence* (*Massiah*) or (4) was the *fruit of other illegal conduct*

COURTROOM IDENTIFICATIONS — an in-court ID is inadmissible if it is the fruit of an *unnecessarily suggestive* pretrial ID procedure conducive to *irreparable mistaken identification*

3. APPLICABILITY OF FOURTH AMENDMENT

INDISCREET CONFIDANTS — D "assumes the risk" that any person he talks to will (1) elicit and report "private" conversations or (2) transmit or tape record the conversation. Thus, no probable cause or warrant is required. *Hoffa v US* (1966); *US v White* (1971).

BANK RECORDS — no reasonable expectation of privacy with regard to checks, deposit slips and other bank records as depositor takes "the risk" in revealing his private affairs to another that the information will be conveyed to the gov't. Thus, gov't may subpoena records without probable cause or warrant. *US v Miller* (1976) — California Supreme Court contra.

NO REASONABLE EXPECTATION OF PRIVACY

VOICE EXEMPLARS — no reasonable expectation that others will not know the sound of D's voice; thus, grand jury may subpoena voice exemplars without probable cause or warrant. *US v Dionisio* (1973).

DISCARDED OR ABANDONED PROPERTY — one has no privacy interest in property he discards or premises he abandons. Some courts forbid inspection of garbage until it is commingled in a common trash receptacle. **Note:** police cannot trespass to obtain evidence if it is discarded.

ELECTRONIC DEVICES — one has no reasonable expectation of privacy in the telephone numbers dialed; thus, police may install a "pen register" to record numbers called without probable cause or warrant. *Smith v Maryland* (1979); police may also place an electronic transmitting device for tracking on packages or cars without probable cause. *US v Knotts* (1983).

DOG SNIFFS — the use of dogs to sniff for drugs is permissible without probable cause or warrant of luggage in police custody. *US v Place* (1983).

PLAIN VIEW (FROM LAWFUL VANTAGE POINT). Plurality in *Coolidge v N.H.* (1971); evidence must be discovered "*inadvertently.*" Plurality in *Texas v Brown* (1983); evidentiary nature need not be "immediately apparent."

PUBLIC PLACE — observations made from a public place do not entail any invasion of privacy unless police use a very sophisticated mechanical device (e.g., long range parabolic microphone) which goes beyond reasonable expectations; use of flashlights, binoculars and other ordinary sense-enhancement devices are permitted.

PRIVATE OPEN AREAS — trespassory entry onto a private open area (e.g., a field) involves no significant intrusion of privacy and observations made therefrom are proper without probable cause or warrant.

CONSENT TO PRIVATE PLACE — if police obtain access to the "vantage point" by voluntary consent, D waives constitutional expectations of privacy to matters observed.

POLICE INVENTORIES — if police have a lawful right to inventory property in their possession, observations made during the reasonable exercise of that right are proper without additional cause or justification.

JUSTIFIABLE INTRUSIONS — if police or others have a legal right to enter a premise for any lawful purpose (e.g., pursuant to a warrant, "hot pursuit" of felon, response to call for help, inspection for damage or dangerous conditions), observations made during the reasonable exercise of this right are lawful without additional cause.

FRISK INCIDENT TO LAWFUL STOP — where there is a lawful right for a limited search (e.g., a surface "pat down"), police may enter inner clothing if they "feel" items which are "probably" weapons.

(continued)

3. APPLICABILITY OF FOURTH AMENDMENT *(continued)*

CONSENT TO A SEARCH OR ENTRY

SCOPE OF CONSENT — consenting party controls scope of the intrusion and conduct exceeding the reasonable scope of the consent is unlawful.

MUST BE VOLUNTARY — under "totality of circumstances" the consent must be *voluntary*; actual or implied coercion is forbidden but deceit does not vitiate consent unless it is extreme (e.g., consent to search based on false representation that officer possesses a warrant). *Bumper v North Carolina* (1968); police not required to inform a suspect that he need not consent, *Schneckloth v Bustamonte* (1973), even if suspect is in custody, *US v Watson* (1976) — N.Y. is contra in certain cases.

IMPLIED CONSENT — statutes which *require* a person to consent to search "at any time" as a condition of a license to engage in certain regulated activities (e.g., dealing in drugs, firearms, cigarettes) are *valid unless unreasonable*; consent to a baggage search may also be implied as a condition to travel by air or to cross U.S. borders.

ADVANCE CONSENT — *explicit prior consent* (e.g., contract provision) to permit searches of rented lockers or premises is valid if not made under duress and if D knew he was consenting; a probationer or parolee may be required to give advance consent for police search as a condition of probation or parole.

THIRD PARTY CONSENT — a search is reasonable if consent was given by any person who has *joint use or access* to the property or premises searched; D assumes the risk that a person who has the right to have or use property will permit others to do so, *US v Matlock* (1974). Reasonable good faith belief that the person consenting had authority (i.e., "apparent authority") will probably be sufficient.

4. VALID WARRANT

NEUTRAL MAGISTRATE — warrant must be issued by a *neutral judicial officer*, *Shadwick v Tampa* (1972).

SUPPORTED BY OATH — facts supporting warrant must be given under oath whether by oral testimony or affidavit. If D makes substantial showing that affiant lied or was reckless re: truth, hearing must be held to determine validity of probable cause and warrant, *Franks v Delaware* (1975).

INDEPENDENT JUDGMENT — facts stated must be in sufficient detail to permit magistrate to make an *independent judgment* that the search will yield the specified evidence, for *"mere conclusions" are improper*, *Riggin v Virginia* (1966).

SPECIFICITY — warrant must specifically limit intrusion by specifically describing items or persons to be seized and/or place to be searched; technical mistakes (e.g., wrong street number) normally *not fatal if* officer cannot mistake the place to be searched; place searched may be owned by non-suspect (including a newspaper) *Zurcher v Stanford Daily* (1978); warrant to search for contraband implicitly carries authority to detain occupants, *Michigan v Summers* (1981); vague warrant cannot be saved by personal supervision of magistrate, *Loli Sales v New York* (1979).

PROBABLE CAUSE

QUANTUM OF PROOF

Traditional Warrant — must be *more probable than not* that purpose of warrant will be accomplished.

Special Administrative Warrants — while prior judicial approval is required to justify an unconsented entry and search to administer *building codes or health regulations*, officer need only show general "area probable cause"; reasonableness requires a balance of interest of state against seriousness of invasion of privacy, *Camara v Municipal Court* (1967); *See v Seattle* (1967).

Identification Evidence —special warrant issued on less than probable cause may be permitted for acquisition of fingerprints, *Davis v Mississippi* (1969).

INFORMATION MUST NOT BE STALE

EXPERIENCE OF AFFIANT MAY BE A FACTOR

BASED ON HEARSAY — strict "two pror g" test of *Aguilar v US* (1964) replaced by more liberal "totality of circumstances": test, *Illinois v Gates* (1983).

Reliability of Informant — If warrant is based on unnamed source or a professional tipster, court will consider the reliability of informant established by *specific facts*, such as previous information which was verified; *ordinary citizens* and *fellow officers* are presumed reliable as are declarations against penal interest.

Basis and Detail of Informer's Knowledge — Even an anonymous informant's information may be sufficient where it is detailed and apparently based on personal knowledge.

Statement of Underlying Facts — magistrate must be told of specific facts known by informant so he can make an independent judgment.

Corroboration — in close cases, courts require that some significant portion of informant's story be verified.

(continued)

4. VALID WARRANT *(continued)*

REASONABLE TIME FROM ISSUANCE — must be executed promptly before probable cause becomes stale.

NIGHTTIME EXECUTION — no Supreme Court limitations, but look to local statutes and overall reasonableness.

FORCED ENTRY — proper if reasonably necessary but police must give "notice and knock" before entry unless there are exigent circumstances, *Ker v California* (1963). Exclusionary rule does not apply, however, where police fail to knock and announce, *Hudson v Michigan* (2001).

EXECUTION

SEARCH OF PERSONS PRESENT AT PLACE DESCRIBED IN WARRANT — while executing a valid search warrant of a tavern police *may not* frisk patrons simply because of their presence; there must be *articulable suspicion* justifying a weapons frisk, *Ybarra v Illinois* (1979).

SEIZURE OF UNDESCRIBED ITEMS — under the "plain view" doctrine, undescribed evidence may be seized if officer has probable cause to believe item is contraband, stolen or dangerous in itself.

DETENTION INCIDENTAL TO WARRANT — a valid search warrant for contraband implicitly carries with it the limited authority to detain occupants of the premises while a proper search is conducted, *Michigan v Summers* (1981).

5. WARRANTLESS SEARCHES

EXIGENT
CIRCUMSTANCES
AND
"REASONABLE
CAUSE"

NECESSITY BECAUSE OF IMPENDING LOSS OF EVIDENCE — where police *have probable cause to justify a warrant*, but the evidence sought could be lost or destroyed if the search is delayed, a warrantless search and seizure is permitted, *Schmerber v California* (1966) — blood alcohol of suspected drunk driver; *US v Van Leeowen* (1970) — luggage or mail in transit.

DURING HOT PURSUIT — search of premises without warrant by officers in *hot pursuit* of a robber still at large is valid, *Warden v Hayden* (1967). But a state statute authorizing blanket warrantless search of a "murder scene" is unconstitutional, *Mincey v Arizona* (1978).

VEHICLES STOPPED ON PUBLIC HIGHWAY — police may stop and search any vehicle on the open highway; if there is probable cause to believe that contraband will be found, *US v Harris* (1968). Search need not actually be made at time of stop or on the highway, it may be made later at the station if driver is taken into custody and car lawfully in police custody, *Chambers v Maroney* (1970). Police may also search suitcases or other separate closed containers found in the vehicle, *US v Ross* (1982).

VEHICLE SEIZED FROM PUBLIC PLACE — above justification was extended to a vehicle parked in *a public parking lot where access was not meaningfully restricted*, *Cardwell v Lewis* (1974).

INVESTIGATORY STOPS AND DETENTIONS — police may stop and detain a person for questioning if there is *reasonable suspicion* (more than hunch, less than probable cause) to believe that the person is committing, has committed or is about to commit a crime, *Terry v Ohio* (1969). Auto may be stopped if there is *articulable reasonable suspicion* that it is unregistered, the driver is unlicensed, or that either the driver or auto is subject to seizure for violation of the law, *Delaware v Prouse* (1979). Police may *stop* and *ask for* ID without reasonable suspicion of criminal conduct, *Brown v Texas* (1979); but suspect may not be arrested for failing to provide "credible and reliable" identification, *Kolender v Lawson* (1983); police may not hold a person's plane ticket and *require* him to accompany them to a private room without probable cause, *Florida v Royer* (1983).

FELONY ARREST — a suspected *felon* may be arrested at any time without a warrant if there is *probable cause* and the suspect is in any *public place*, *US v Watson* (1976). But an arrest warrant is required to enter and effectuate a *routine felony arrest* inside the suspect's own home, *Payton v New York* (1980); though if police see a person in her doorway they may follow her into the home immediately to make the arrest, *US v Santana* (1976). It is not unreasonable for an officer to monitor the movements of an arrested person by entering D's room where D was allowed by officer to enter to get ID, *Washington v Chrisman* (1982).

(continued)

5. WARRANTLESS SEARCHES *(continued)*

SEARCHES AND SEIZURES INCIDENT TO OTHER LAWFUL CONDUCT

LAWFUL INVENTORY — police may take a full inventory of the contents of D's property (including vehicles) lawfully in police possession in order to (1) safeguard D's property and (2) protect police against false claims of theft and evidence observed in plain view during inventory may be seized, *South Dakota v Opperman* (1976). No additional cause of any kind is required and an inventory of the contents of any container (e.g., valise, box, wallet) possessed by an arrestee may be taken; there is no requirement that they seal and store the container as is, *Illinois v LaFayette* (1983).

LAWFUL STOP — a suspect may be "frisked" if police have reasonable suspicion that he is armed and dangerous, *Terry v Ohio* (1969). But mere presence at a place being lawfully searched is not enough; police must have articulable and reasonable suspicion that persons searched are armed or have evidence, *Ybarra v Illinois* (1979). However, if police lawfully stop a driver they may "frisk" his person **and** the passenger compartment of the car even if alternative means of assuring safety are available, *Michigan v Long* (1983).

LAWFUL ARREST — D and his "immediate presence" may be searched incident to a lawful arrest

Scope — includes D and everything within D's "reach" to protect officer and to prevent destruction of evidence by D, *Chinel v California* (1969). Some cases dilute limitation by "lunge doctrine," by allowing search of handcuffed D or "sweep search" of area for another person. Jacket of suspect found in back seat could be searched, *New York v Belton* (1981).

Timing — must be substantially contemporaneous to arrest but may precede arrest slightly, *US v Chadwick* (1977).

Crime — full search of arrested person is justified regardless of the crime giving rise to the arrest; even traffic arrests (though some states contra), *US v Robinson* (1973).

BORDER SEARCHES

AT BORDER — merely crossing a US border (or its functional equivalent) justifies a search and/or seizure of person, luggage or mail without cause.

FIXED CHECKPOINTS — vehicles may be "stopped" without cause at a fixed checkpoint in the vicinity of the border, but police must have probable cause to fully search the vehicle, *US v Martinez-Fuerte* (1976).

ROVING PATROLS — vehicles may be "stopped" if police have reasonable suspicion, but search requires probable cause, *US v Almeida-Sanchez* (1973); *US v Brigmono-Ponce* (1975).

SEARCHES IN FOREIGN COUNTRIES — the Fourth Amendment does not apply to searches and seizures in foreign countries by U.S. authorities. Evidence so obtained may be admitted.

6. STATEMENTS AND CONFESSIONS

INVOLUNTARY STATEMENTS

— compelled statements violate the Fifth Amendment right against self incrimination; *involuntariness* is viewed in the *totality of circumstances.*

PHYSICAL FORCE — virtually any use of force to extract a statement will disqualify a statement.

PROMISES AND TRICKS — police are given broad leeway to trick and deceive during interrogation but extreme cases of falsely playing on suspect's sympathies and promises of leniency in return for a confession can justify treating statement as involuntary, *Spano v New York* (1959).

UNCONSCIOUSNESS — statements taken from a semiconscious D are improper, *Mincey v Arizona* (1978).

LOSS OF JOB — statements elicited from a public employee under threats of discharge are involuntary.

CUSTODY — occurs when suspect is deprived of freedom of action *in any significant way* (more than "stop" or brief detention but not necessarily an arrest; examine from police point of view: was there a *manifestation of intended control* (statement by D to his probation officer without warnings was O.K. since D was not in custody when questions were asked, *Minnesota v Murphy* (1984).

MIRANDA RULE

— a suspect who is in *custody* may not be *interrogated* unless he is first told that: (1) he has a *right to remain silent,* (2) that *statements made will be used against him,* (3) that he has a *right to the presence of an attorney,* and (4) that *if he can't afford an attorney one will be appointed.*

INTERROGATION
— warnings need only be given if police interrogate (i.e., attempt to elicit an incriminating response).

Spontaneous Statements — *Miranda* does not apply to unsolicited spontaneous confessions or "blurted out" statements.

Conduct — interrogation includes conduct which police know is reasonably likely to elicit an incriminating response especially if police play on known weaknesses of D, *Rhode Island v Innis* (1980).

ASSERTION OR WAIVER
— suspect may either assert any of the rights encompassed in warning or waive them.

Assertion — once asserted all interrogation must cease immediately and a subsequent waiver from subsequent but proximately close interrogation is improper, *Edwards v Arizona* (1981), unless clearly done in good faith by different officers, *Michigan v Mosley* (1976). Request for a person other than an attorney such as a mother or probation officer is *not* an assertion of the right to silence, *Fare v Michael C* (1979).

Waiver — state must prove *knowing and intelligent waiver*; prosecution carries "heavy burden" but waiver need not be explicit or written, *North Carolina v Butler* (1979).

FORM OF WARNINGS — no ritualistic form is required as long as substance is clear but warnings must be given to every suspect — even police and hardened criminals, *North Carolina v Butler* (1974).

USE — an actual statement taken in violation of Miranda may be used to impeach direct testimony, *Harris v New York* (1971); but the fact that D asserted his right to silence and failed to explain may *not* be used to impeach credibility of court testimony, *US v Hale* (1975) unless D's pre-arrest silence is *clearly inconsistent* with defense asserted at trial, *Jenkins v Anderson* (1980).

RIGHT TO COUNSEL: MASSIAH — once *formal charges have been filed* and D has a lawyer, incriminating statements may not be elicited from D without a clear waiver of the right to counsel; this is so whether D is in custody or not.

On Bail — surreptitiously recorded conversation by secret police agent while D was out on bail violated right to counsel, *Massiah v US* (1964).

If Asserted — once right to counsel is asserted, all attempts to elicit statements must cease, *Brewer v Williams* (1977).

FRUIT OF ILLEGAL CONDUCT — a statement or confession may be suppressed if it was fruit of any prior unconstitutional conduct such as an illegal search and seizure or identification procedure even if statement itself was voluntary and given after valid waiver of *Miranda* and *Massiah* rights. *NOTE:* D must have standing to object to the source illegality.

7. IDENTIFICATION PROCEDURES

SELF-INCRIMINATION — Fifth Amendment privilege against self-incrimination only applies to *testimonial communicative evidence* not physical evidence. Thus, a suspect may be compelled to participate in a fair line-up, provide hair, blood or voice samples and to put on or remove clothes, toupees, etc., *Schmerber v California* (1966); *Wade v US* (1967).

RIGHT TO COUNSEL — once formal charges have been brought, a suspect has a right to the presence of counsel at any line-up, *Kirby v Illinois* (1972); but not at photographic displays, *US v Ash* (1973). The right to counsel at this stage may be waived, *Wade v US* (1967). [Omnibus Crime Control Act seeking to override cases holding a right to counsel at a line-up is probably unconstitutional. In N.Y., suspect has a *non-waivable* right to counsel at a post-charge line-up, *P v Settles* (1978).]

DUE PROCESS — an I.D. procedure is violative of Due Process when it is "(1) *unnecessarily* (2) *suggestive* and (3) *conducive to irreparable mistaken identification;*" any in-court I.D. tainted thereby is inadmissible, *Stovall v Denno* (1967).

TOTALITY OF CIRCUMSTANCES — in determining whether in-court I.D. is the "fruit" of the pretrial I.D. consider (1) witness's opportunity to observe criminal at time of the act; (2) witness's degree of attention; (3) accuracy and specificity of witness's prior description, and (4) the level of certainty of witness, *Neil v Briggers* (1972).

HEARING — hearing must be held as to propriety of pretrial I.D. but need not be outside the presence of the jury, *Watkins v Sowders* (1981).

PHOTOGRAPHIC DISPLAYS — only factors which are unnecessarily suggestive will taint a photo I.D. (e.g., repetitive display of same photo, circle or marks on photo, etc.).

LINE-UP — persons must be of similar but not identical physical characteristics; particular suspect must not unduly stand out or otherwise be pointed to by prosecution or police, *Foster v California* (1969) — D only person to be in two separate line-ups and to wear jacket similar to one worn by robbers.

ONE PERSON SHOW-UPS — not violative *per se* if justified by special circumstances.

8. RIGHT TO COUNSEL

SIXTH AMENDMENT — the Sixth Amendment right to counsel applies at all *critical stages* of a *criminal proceeding*.

Criminal Proceeding — hearings on trials *after* the state "is committed to prosecution" *through disposition and sentencing (excludes* grand jury proceedings, probable cause hearings and post-sentencing/conviction proceedings) including *petty offenses if actual jail sentence is imposed, Kirby v Illinois* (1972); *Argersinger v Hamlin* (1972); *Scott v Illinois* (1979).

Critical Stages — where substantial rights of the accused are at stake: (1) *preliminary examinations*; (2) *custodial interrogation*; (3) *post indictment interrogation*; (4) *post indictment line-up*; (5) *arraignment* (only if D pleads guilty or statute requires that certain defense be raised); (6) *sentencing*.

BASIS OF RIGHT

DUE PROCESS — the due process clause of the Fifth and Fourteenth Amendments may require a right to counsel.

Juvenile Proceedings —juvenile has a due process right to counsel in any proceeding "which *may* result in commitment to an institution," *In re Gault* (1967).

Probation and Parole Revocation — due process requires a fair hearing with "adversarial safeguards; right to counsel considered on a case by case basis considering (1) *seriousness of consequences*, (2) *complexity of issues* and (3) *accused's competence to protect rights*, *Gaghon v Scarpelli* (1973).

EQUAL PROTECTION — an *indigent* accused has a constitutional right to *appointed counsel* under the equal protection clause.

On Appeal — If state permits appeal *as matter of right,* counsel must be provided to an indigent, *Douglas v California* (1963) and counsel must write the best brief she can, *Anders v California* (1967).

Other Situations — accused does *not* have an equal protection right to counsel in all cases where a person who could afford an attorney could be represented, *Ross v Moffit* (1974); but counsel must be provided at all critical stages of a criminal proceeding (Sixth Amendment right to counsel).

Indigence — accused is unable to obtain necessary assistance *without substantial hardship;* it is constitutional to require reimbursement at a later time, *Fuller v Oregon* (1974).

(continued)

8. RIGHT TO COUNSEL *(continued)*

Farce or Mockery — general view is still that reversal is necessary only when the trial was reduced to a "farce or mockery of justice" though modern trend moves toward a standard of "reasonable competence."

Conflict of Interest — if a true and genuine conflict of interests results from joint representation of two defendants, counsel is constitutionally ineffective.

NATURE OF RIGHT
— **"EFFECTIVE" COUNSEL** — counsel must be *competent.*

Restricted Counsel — denial of final argument or order to prevent accused from conferring with counsel during recess violates right to effective counsel.

Meaningful Relationship — D does not have a right to a "meaningful attorney-client privilege" so long as appointed counsel is competent, *Morris v Slappy* (1983).

Plain Error Alternative — where "competent" counsel fails to object causing a plain and manifest injustice (i.e., plain error), court must reverse to preserve accused's constitutional rights.

WAIVER — the right to counsel may be waived "knowingly and intelligently."

Accused Must Be Clearly Competent to Waive.

Proceeding Pro Se — accused has right to represent self, *Faretta v California* (1975).

1. OVERVIEW: PROPHES

P – Probative Sufficiency   **R** – Reliability   **O** – Opinion   **P** – Privilege   **H** – Hearsay   **E** – Examination   **S** – Substitutes for Evidence

LOGICAL RELEVANCY
– must have some tendency to prove or disprove a fact of consequence.

PROBATIVE SUFFICIENCY
– must be sufficiently probative to warrant admission.

LEGAL RELEVANCY
– may not be substantially more prejudicial than probative.

Similar Happenings and Transactions – proponent must show a *substantial identity of material circumstances.*

Absence of Similar Happenings (Negative Evidence) – proponent must show (1) a *substantial identity of material circumstances* and that (2) *happening would have been known by witness if it occurred.*

Foundation (Authentication and Identification) – proponent must offer *sufficient evidence to sustain a finding that the evidence* (e.g., a writing, physical object, or voice) is *what its proponent purports it to be.* FRE allows self-authentication in some cases.

Liability Insurance – inadmissible to prove negligence, but may prove disputed ownership or control and bias of witness or potential juror.

Settlements and Compromises (Including Offers) – to encourage out-of-court settlements, inadmissible as an admission of fault or to establish value of claim, but may explain delay or show bias.

Subsequent Remedial Measures – to encourage safety measures, inadmissible to prove negligence, but may prove disputed ownership or control and, under modern trend, that there was a *defect* for strict liability.

Character Evidence – *reputation, specific instances of conduct, or personal opinion* bearing on character or propensity is inadmissible to prove conduct consistent therewith except if *habit* or, in criminal cases only, if *mercy rule or prosecutor's rule* applies. May be used to prove (1) *character, if an essential element of the case;* (2) relevant *knowledge of another's character,* or (3) to *impeach a testifying witness* (subject to limitations on extrinsic evidence).

Impeachment – witness may be asked questions which tend to discredit (intrinsic impeachment), but *extrinsic evidence of bad character may be used to impeach only if in the form of conviction or it is relevant to a material matter beyond witness credibility.*

(continued)

1. OVERVIEW: PROPHES *(continued)*

RELIABILITY – must meet a minimal threshold of trustworthiness.

WITNESS COMPETENCY – FRE abandons mental and moral prerequisites, defects go to weight, common law disqualifies a witness if court finds witness cannot (1) *accurately recount the facts and give meaningful testimony*, or (2) *understand the significance of the obligation to tell the truth.*

SCIENTIFIC DEVICES AND TESTS – proponent must establish that (1) device or theory is *recognized and accepted in the relevant scientific community;* (2) the *device used was in proper working order;* and (3) *device was operated and interpreted by a qualified person.*

BEST EVIDENCE RULE (ORIGINAL WRITING RULE) – when the *contents of a writing are in issue*, the *original* (includes reliable photocopy under FRE) must be *produced* or shown to be *unavailable.* Contents are in issue if (1) writing has independent legal significance, (2) proponent offers a writing, or (3) witness testimony is dependent on the contents of writing.

DEADMAN'S ACT – *abandoned under FRE* and many states; where it applies, it prevents testimony as to a transaction with a now deceased or incompetent party unless the testimony is corroborated by independent evidence.

OPINION

LAY OPINION – non-experts may give *sensory opinions* within common experience so long as there is a sufficient opportunity to perceive; quasi-experts may give moderate expert-type opinions if sufficient foundation is laid.

EXPERT OPINION – expert opinion may be given if (1) it *assists the fact finder* (many states require that the opinion be *necessary,* i.e., relate to matters beyond common understanding), (2) the witness is *qualified as an expert,* and (3) the opinion is *within the state of the art of the field of expertise.* May be based on matters not in evidence and inadmissible matter if of the type relied on by reasonable experts: expert may be cross-examined regarding contents of authoritative treatise (common law requires reliance).

PRIVILEGE

RELATIONSHIP – communication must be made as part of a statutorily designated relationship, no requirement of fee or acceptance of case if communicator was seeking professional advice or treatment. Minority view – reasonable belief that relationship exists is sufficient.

COMMUNICATION – except in special circumstances, only verbal communications are protected, not observations or impressions (but separate *spousal privilege* prevents testimony as to any matter, not just revelation of confidential communication).

CONFIDENTIALITY – presence of inessential person not otherwise privileged precludes privilege (persons who advance the purpose of the privilege such as doctors or investigators employed to aid a lawyer are protected by privilege).

HOLDER – only holder may waive privilege, privilege may be asserted by another *on holder's behalf,* but holder controls.

WAIVER – holder permanently loses privilege as to communications voluntarily revealed by him or by another if holder fails to object when he had an opportunity to do so.

EXCEPTIONS – privilege not available in suits between persons in the protected relationship; joint clients or where communication was made to advance a crime or fraud.

1. OVERVIEW: PROPHES *(continued)*

HEARSAY

EXCLUSIONS – out-of-court assertion *admissible for a relevant purpose not dependent on its truth:* (1) state of mind of the declarant or listener (2) prior statement to impeach, or (3) rehabilitate verbal event.

EXEMPTIONS – under the FRE, certain out-of-court statements are not hearsay even when used to prove their truth: (1) *admissions,* (2) *prior I.D. of a testifying witness,* (3) *prior sworn statements inconsistent with courtroom testimony;* (4) *prior consistent statements used to rebut inference of recent fabrication or undue influence.*

EXCEPTIONS – Admissions, Declaration against interest, Dying declaration, Excited utterance, Mental state exception. Physical sensation. Business record, Official written statement, Past recollection recorded, Prior recorded testimony. Sense impressions, Expert exception, Equivalency exception.

EXAMINATION

DIRECT EXAMINATION – look out for: (1) leading, (2) narrative, (3) assuming facts, (4) compound, and (5) argumentative.

CROSS-EXAMINATION – must generally be within scope of direct exam; leading questions proper.

SUBSTITUTES FOR EVIDENCE

JUDICIAL NOTICE – no formal proof required for: (1) state and federal laws and regulations; (2) universally known facts, or (3) facts subject to undisputed verification.

PRESUMPTIONS – directs the jury's fact finding process by a special instruction; *FRE and majority – presumption only shifts burden of producing evidence to party opposing presumed fact;* in some states, certain presumptions based on a strong public policy shift burden of persuasion to opponent of presumed fact.

2. LOGICAL RELEVANCY

CIRCUMSTANTIAL EVIDENCE – fact to be proved must be inferred from other facts; admissible if it has *some tendency to prove or disprove a fact of consequence*. Is fact to be proved more likely with the evidence than it was without it?

SIMILAR ACCIDENTS OR INJURIES – may prove dangerousness of a particular condition or knowledge of that condition by prior or subsequent similar happenings if a *substantial identity of all material circumstances is shown* – burden is on proponent to lay foundation.

SIMILAR CONTRACTS OR TRANSACTIONS – to prove or clarify the terms of a transaction or agreement, proponent may offer evidence of similar but unrelated transactions with opposing party, but not with third parties (some cases have allowed third party evidence as court has broad discretion).

NEGATIVE EVIDENCE – proponent may prove that other similar happenings did *not* occur to prove safety of a particular condition or no notice if proponent shows (1) *a substantial identity of material circumstances* with respect to evidence, and (2) *that happening would have been observed by witness if it had occurred.*

OTHER INFERENCES MAY BE EQUALLY OR MORE PLAUSIBLE – evidence need only have *some tendency* to prove fact sought; close questions tend to be resolved in favor of admission.

WRITINGS

CONNECTING EVIDENCE (AUTHENTICATION OR IDENTIFICATION) – evidence must be authenticated or identified as a condition precedent to admissibility by the offer of preliminary facts sufficient to support a finding that the matter in question is what its proponent claims. FRE 901(a).

Personal Knowledge – testimony from any witness with personal knowledge that the writing was prepared by the person claimed. FRE 901(b)(1).

Identification of Handwriting – non-expert opinion as to genuineness based on familiarity not acquired for purposes of litigation, FRE 901(b)(2), or comparison with an authenticated exemplar by a qualified expert or the trier of fact. FRE 901(b)(3).

Circumstantial Evidence – evidence indicating that information revealed or matters stated in the writing tend to identify the source as a particular person or firm (sometimes called the "reply message" doctrine), based on notion that the contents, *other than direct statements* of self-identification such as signatures or letterheads, if unique, can create a sufficient inference as to who prepared the writing. Do not confuse with forms of self-authentication. FRE 901(b)(4).

Public Records or Reports – evidence that a purported public record was in the custody of the proper public office. FRE 901(b)(7). Includes electronic data.

Ancient Writing – evidence that a writing (1) is in such a condition as to create no suspicion regarding its authenticity, (2) was in a place where, if authentic, it should likely be, *and* (3) it is at least 20 years old. FRE 901(8). Common law required 30 years. Note, there is also a hearsay exception for properly authenticated ancient writings. FRE 803(16).

Self-Authentication – extrinsic evidence of authenticity is not required with respect to a number of special writings including (1) *public documents* if sealed or certified, (2) *official publications* purportedly issued by public authority, (3) *newspapers and periodicals* indicating publisher, (4) *trade inscriptions* such as tags, labels, or signs purporting to indicate origin, ownership, or control, and which were affixed in the course of business, (5) *acknowledged documents*, (6) *commercial paper*, and (7) *documents identified by statutory presumption.* FRE 902.

VOICES

Personal Knowledge – testimony from any witness who heard the statement, saw the speaker, and has personal knowledge of the identity of the speaker. FRE 901(b)(1).

Identification of Voice – where speaker is unseen or unknown, an opinion identifying a voice based upon hearing the voice under circumstances connecting it with the alleged speaker (whether heard first-hand, by recording, or telephone), or by comparison by an expert or the trier of fact with an authenticated exemplar of the voice. FRE 901(b)(3), (4).

Distinctive Characteristics – evidence of unique contents, internal patterns, or other distinctive characteristics (e.g., accent) taken in conjunction with the circumstances. FRE 901(b)(4).

Special Rule for Telephone Conversations – in addition to the above methods, a *person can be identified by evidence that (1) a telephone call was made to a number assigned to that person by the telephone company*, and (2) *circumstances including self-identification*, show the person answering to be the one called. FRE 901(b)(6)(A). In the case of a *business*, (1) evidence that a *call was made to a number assigned to the business by the telephone company*, and (2) *the conversation related to business reasonably transacted over the telephone.* FRE 901(b)(6)(B).

PHYSICAL OBJECTS – physical objects such as guns, heroin, etc., may be identified as above including: (1) *personal knowledge* – testimony recognizing the object to be what it purports to be; (2) *distinctive characteristics or markings*; and (3) *chain of possession* – testimony accounting for objects' whereabouts from point of incident at issue until trial (must also show no likelihood of tampering).

3. LEGAL RELEVANCY

Otherwise relevant evidence is inadmissible if, taken as a whole, its probative value is substantially outweighed by the danger of (1) unfair prejudice, (2) confusion of the issues, (3) misleading the jury, or by (4) considerations of undue delay, waste of time, or needless presentation of cumulative evidence. FRE 403.

DISCRETIONARY EXCLUSION

TYPICAL PROBLEMS – *gruesome evidence* (e.g., gory color photos, blood-stained objects), *statistical probabilities, prior bad acts used to impeach a criminal defendant-witness* (even if permitted under character and impeachment rules).

FACTORS

- **LIMITING INSTRUCTION** – is it likely that cautionary instruction will protect against improper inference?

- **ALTERNATIVES** – are there less offensive ways of proving the same facts available to proponent?

- **MATERIALITY** – is the evidence directed toward a critical central issue or merely toward background or corroborative facts? (The more important the evidence, the more likely it is to be admitted since probative value is higher.)

- **NATURE OF RISK** – will admission of the evidence create a risk of convicting an innocent person? (Exclusion is most likely upon objection of a criminal defendant.)

(continued)

3. LEGAL RELEVANCY *(continued)*

MANDATORY EXCLUSION

Special statutory or common law rules specifically prohibiting certain forms of evidence to be used to prove certain facts.

LIABILITY INSURANCE – *evidence that a person was or was not insured for liability at the time of an injury is inadmissible for the purpose of proving that such person acted negligently or wrongfully*. Admissible to prove other relevant facts: (1) *agency*, (2) *ownership or control* (if disputed), (3) *bias or prejudice of a witness* (e.g., witness employed by insurance company liable for judgment rendered). FRE 411. **Rationale:** evidence tempts fact finder to improperly consider ability-to-pay and possibly "deep pocket" of insurance company.

SUBSEQUENT REMEDIAL MEASURES
– *evidence of a remedial measure, taken or authorized by a civil defendant after the occurrence of an injury, is inadmissible for the purpose of proving negligence or culpable conduct of the defendant.* Admissible to prove other relevant facts: (1) *ownership or control* (if disputed), (2) *feasibility of precautionary measures* (if disputed), and (3) *impeachment* of defendant's testimony. FRE 407. **Rationale:** to encourage persons to make products and premises as safe as they can be made by removing chance that remedial act will be used as an admission.

REMEDIAL MEASURE – includes repairs, changes in procedure, termination or additional training of employee, adoption of rule or other improvement tending to make a product or condition safer.

PRODUCTS LIABILITY ACTION – recent state cases hold that rule does *not* bar use of evidence of subsequent design changes as evidence of "defect" in a products liability case since cause of action does not require showing of negligence or culpable conduct.

ACTUAL OR ATTEMPTED COMPROMISE
– *evidence respecting an actual settlement of a disputed claim or an attempt to compromise such claim (including any statement made during compromise negotiations) is inadmissible to prove the validity or value of the claim.* Admissible to prove other relevant facts: (1) *bias of a witness*, (2) *explain delay* (if undue delay is claimed), and (3) *obstruction of justice.* FRE 408. **Rationale:** to encourage out-of-court settlement of disputes.

FINAL SETTLEMENT – rule only excludes statements or acts directed at a final resolution of a dispute; it does *not* exclude payments of or offers to pay for damages unless meant as a mutually binding settlement (see below re: medical expenses).

EXCLUDES EXPLICIT ADMISSIONS – *contra to common law,* the FRE bars all statements made during good faith compromise discussions.

PAYMENT OR OFFER TO PAY MEDICAL BILLS – *evidence of the payment or offer to pay medical, hospital, or similar expenses resulting from an injury at issue is inadmissible to prove liability for the injury.* FRE 409. Common law has no analog. **Note:** specific admissions not necessary to the offer to pay are admissible. **Rationale:** to encourage Good Samaritan payments.

PLEAS AND OFFERS TO PLEA – *evidence of an offer to plead guilty, nolo contendere or actual pleas later withdrawn (as well as any statements made in connection therewith) are inadmissible in any civil or criminal case.* Such evidence is admissible to impeach testimony or prove perjury, or if in the form of a *voluntary and reliable statement made on the record in court.* FRE 410. **Rationale:** to advance the policies of nolo contendere, plea bargaining, and to make meaningful the judicial decision to allow a plea to be withdrawn.

3. LEGAL RELEVANCY (continued)

CHARACTER EVIDENCE (See Flowchart 4) – *evidence of a person's character is inadmissible to prove conduct on a particular occasion except when it is: (1) in the form of habit (invariable repeated behavior), (2) used to impeach a witness (subject to limitations imposed by impeachment rules), or (3) reputation or personal opinion offered by a criminal defendant to show innocence, or by the prosecutor to rebut such evidence (i.e., the "Mercy Rule") and (4) specific implicating facts not derived from disposition alone* (e.g., motive, opportunity, intent, knowledge, identity, or plan). Admissible (subject to discretionary exclusion discussed above) for relevant purposes other than proving conduct: (1) *character or reputation as a primary issue*, and (2) *knowledge of character or disposition*. FRE 404. **Rationale:** to prevent undue prejudice caused by a focus on the character of a person rather than the particular facts of the litigation.

EXTRINSIC IMPEACHMENT: COLLATERAL MATTER RULE

– *evidence not elicited on cross-examination from a witness himself is inadmissible to impeach that witness unless the impeachment goes to a material matter and, in certain cases, the witness has been, or will be afforded, an opportunity to explain or deny the evidence.* **Rationale:** credibility with respect to a nonmaterial fact is collateral; extrinsic evidence only tending to discredit on a collateral matter may confuse the issues, mislead the jury, and consume an undue amount of time.

MATERIALITY – evidence must either tend to discredit (1) the testimony as a whole by showing *bias, defects in perception or memory, or untrustworthy character* (manifested by a conviction), or (2) testimony about an outcome-affecting fact as by showing a material *inconsistent statement.*

CONFRONTATION – in order to make extrinsic impeachment a last resort, proponent normally required to confront the witness with the evidence *prior* to the offer, however, under FRE 613(b), it is sufficient to permit confrontation after the evidence is admitted. No confrontation is required for the use of convictions.

CONTRADICTION – evidence admissible on a substantive issue (i.e., other than impeachment) may be offered extrinsically regardless of its tendency to discredit a previous witness (this is so even at common law where a party may not impeach his own witness).

MINORITY RULE – some states (e.g., California) reject Collateral Matter Rule and permit extrinsic evidence on any substantive or credibility issue.

4. CHARACTER EVIDENCE

GENERAL RULE: Evidence of a Person's Character or Disposition is Inadmissible Proof of the Conduct of that Person on a Particular Occasion Except as Otherwise Permitted by Law.

ISSUE SPOTTING SEQUENCE: (1) Is the evidence a form of character evidence? (2) Is the evidence admissible to prove factors other than conduct? (3) If used to prove conduct, is the evidence admissible under a specific exception to the general rule?

(1) FORMS.

REPUTATION – Evidence purporting to state the community reputation of a person (P); witness need not actually know P.

PERSONAL OPINION – Evidence which includes a personal opinion (as opposed to community opinion) of P's character or disposition; witness must actually know P.

OTHER ACTS – Evidence of acts done by P either prior or subsequent to the conduct at issue in the case.

(2) NON-CONDUCT USES – Character evidence is not excluded by the general rule if its relevancy is not dependent on proving specific conduct of the person characterized.

CHARACTER AS AN ULTIMATE ISSUE – All appropriate forms admissible to prove P's character where it is an essential element of: (1) *a cause of action or claim* (e.g., character of parent in child custody action; mental condition of testator in probate dispute); (2) a *defense* (e.g., truth in defamation action; insanity in criminal case); or (3) *the existence or amount of damages* (e.g., reputation before and after alleged injury). FRE 405.

KNOWLEDGE OF CHARACTER – If the use of character evidence is limited to proving that one person knew or should have known of the character of another (P), e.g., *negligent entrustment, self-defense*), all appropriate forms are admissible. If used to test the knowledge and qualifications of a reputation witness regarding P, questions may be asked of witness on cross-examination as to whether he "had heard" of specific acts of P which would bear on reputation – questions must be asked in good faith; acts may not be too remote to affect P's present reputation; court may exclude if P is a party and the question is more prejudicial than probative.

– 82 –

KAPLAN) *pmbr*

4. CHARACTER EVIDENCE *(continued)*

CHARACTER OF ACCUSED (MERCY RULE) – An accused may offer either good reputation or personal opinion (but *not* specific acts) which tends to prove her innocence in a criminal case. If accused does offer good character evidence, prosecutor may rebut by evidence of bad character (but only in the form of reputation or opinion). Common law only permits reputation. FRE 404(a)(1).

VICTIM'S CHARACTER OFFERED BY ACCUSED – Except in rape cases, an accused may offer evidence of the character of an alleged victim in a criminal case in the form of reputation, opinion or by specific relevant instances of conduct elicited on cross-examination. If accused does offer, prosecutor may rebut. FRE 404(a)(2). In rape cases, reputation or opinion evidence of the victim's past sexual behavior is *not* admissible but evidence of past sexual behavior (i.e., specific acts) may be offered if: (1) acts with person other than accused tend to prove that accused was not the source of semen or injury, *or* (2) past acts with accused tend to show consent. In both cases, accused must make a written motion and offer of proof and court shall conduct an in-chambers hearing to decide whether and to what extent the past sexual behavior will be admitted. FRE 412.

STRONG CIRCUMSTANTIAL EVIDENCE: OTHER ACTS – In a criminal or civil action, any party may prove that a person did a specific act of a particular occasion by character evidence in the form of specific acts if such evidence establishes: (1) *motive*, (2) *opportunity*, (3) *knowledge or intent* (including absence of mistake or accident), (4) *preparation or plan*, or (5) *identity* (as with *modus operandi*). FRE 404(b). Evidence is *not* dependent on "mere disposition" as it closely and specifically links the person to the act in question.

HABIT – Evidence of a person's habit (i.e., invariable automatic pattern of behavior) may be used to prove conduct in conformity to the habit. FRE 406. No need for corroboration. Considered highly probative of conduct (also applies to routine practice of an organization). FRE 406.

(3) EXCEPTIONS – In the following specific situations character evidence may be used to prove conduct because of special considerations which make the evidence more probative than prejudicial.

REPUTATION FOR TRUTH AND VERACITY – Proper to impeach or rehabilitate if witness qualified? no special foundation required.

PERSONAL OPINION – Permitted if witness qualified; no special foundation. FRE 608(a). Common law does *not* permit.

WITNESS' CHARACTER RE: CREDIBILITY – Character evidence may be used to impeach or rehabilitate the testimony of a witness. Admissibility depends on form and whether evidence conforms with impeachment rules (e.g., collateral matter rule).

FELONY CONVICTIONS – Name and fact of conviction of any felony permitted even if underlying crime does *not* involve dishonesty or false statement. May be elicited on cross-exam or proved extrinsically, no special foundation. FRE 609.

MISDEMEANOR CONVICTIONS – Name and fact of conviction permitted but only if underlying crime involves dishonesty or false statement. May be elicited on cross-exam or proved extrinsically, no special foundation. FRE 609. Minority (e.g., California) do not permit at all.

OTHER ACTS {

UNCONVICTED CONDUCT – Witness may be impeached by direct evidence of specific acts by the witness (*not* arrests, indictments, etc.) which bear on truthfulness or honesty, *may be elicited on cross-exam asking if the witness actually did the act, no extrinsic evidence permitted if witness denies act.* FRE 609. Minority (e.g., California) do not permit use of unconvicted conduct.

REVERSED AND UNCONSTITUTIONAL CONVICTIONS – May not be used but if appeal is still pending, use permitted.

JUVENILE CONVICTIONS – May only be used to impeach a prosecution witness in a criminal case, not the defendant or a defense witness.

DISCRETION – Court may always exclude impeaching evidence if it is deemed more prejudicial than probative. If a party is the witness (especially a criminal accused), court will carefully examine the probative value of convictions and other acts to determine relevancy (i.e., does act relate closely enough to truthfulness or honesty, is it too remote?). Convictions over 10 years old must be specifically examined for probative value. FRE 609(b).

5. MINIMAL RELIABILITY

TESTIMONIAL COMPETENCE

OATH OF AFFIRMATION – Witness must declare that he will testify truthfully, by oath or affirmation administered in a form calculated to awaken his conscience and impress his mind with the obligation to do so. FRE 603. At common law, witness must also demonstrate that he understands the obligation to tell the truth.

PERSONAL KNOWLEDGE – A witness may not testify to a matter unless evidence is introduced sufficient to support a finding that he has personal knowledge of the matter. FRE 602.

MENTAL CAPACITY – FRE 601 abandons all common law requirements relating to capacity to perceive and tell the truth. Thus, no witness is incompetent to testify by virtue of age, mental illness (including illness directly related to knowing and telling the truth), use of drugs or alcohol (even if shortly before testifying) or any other fact – all such facts may be used to impeach the witness and go to weight rather than admissibility. Common law is contra requiring, on objection, a special judicial finding that the witness has the capacity to accurately observe, remember, and recount the facts.

FINANCIAL INTEREST IN OUTCOME: DEAD MAN'S RULE – The FRE abandons the common law dead man's rule which disqualifies witnesses who have a financial interest in the outcome of a civil suit (applicable where the opposing party is incapable of testifying because of death or mental incompetency). Many major states (e.g., New York, Florida) still retain such statutes, which differ substantially in specific provisions.

SPECIAL STATUS ──
⎧ **JUDGE AS A WITNESS** – A judge may not testify in any trial in which he is presiding. FRE 605.

JUROR AS A WITNESS – A member of the jury may not testify as a witness in a case in which she is sitting as a juror. FRE 606(a). A juror is also incompetent to testify as to any matter or statement occurring during the course of the jury's deliberations, nor may she testify as to any matter which influences her vote or any other juror's vote even upon an inquiry into the validity of an indictment or verdict. **Exception:** May testify re: *extraneous prejudicial information* brought to jury's attention or whether there was an *improper outside influence*. FRE 606(b).

⎩ **ATTORNEY AS A WITNESS** – Although there are major ethical restrictions regarding the testimony of an attorney, her partner or associate in any case in which she is representing a client, an attorney is *not* incompetent under the evidence rules.

BEST EVIDENCE RULE (BER): EXCLUSION OF SECONDARY EVIDENCE

In (**1**) *proving the contents of a writing*, (**2**) the *original writing itself* (**3**) must be *produced* (**4**) or shown to be *unavailable* (**5**) *by the proponent of the secondary evidence* (**6**) unless the writing refers to a *collateral issue*.

(continued)

5. MINIMAL RELIABILITY *(continued)*

(1) PROVING CONTENTS OF WRITING
– BER only applies when the evidence offered is intended to prove what the writing says; not applicable if evidence merely seeks to establish there was a writing or if the actual precise content of the writing is irrelevant to its evidentiary value.

CONTENTS IN ISSUE

Category 1: Writing Has Independent Legal Significance – Rights or obligations at issue arise from, and are directly affected by, the precise content of the writing. **Examples:** Actions based on a *will, written contract, lease;* liability affected by specific *written notice or disclaimer; defamatory writing, manuscripts and books* in copyright actions; recordings of *defamatory statements or extortionate threats* where action is based on precise words; *photos or motion pictures* in pornography action.

Category 2: Writing Offered as Evidence – Party puts contents of writing in issue by offering it in evidence even if writing is not of independent legal significance. **Examples:** *Receipt* to prove payment; *transcripts or minutes* to prove what was said at prior hearing or meeting; *letters, memos, notes* to prove knowledge, intent, motive or attitude of author or recipient; *x-ray* to prove injury. **(Note:** Writing must also be authenticated and avoid hearsay rule).

Category 3: Testimony Reliant on Writing – Witness puts contents of writing in issue if his testimony is derived from what he saw in a writing, rather than from personal knowledge of the facts evidenced by the writing (i.e., witness is merely a conduit for the writing itself). **Examples:** testimony based upon a letter, x-ray, tape recording, transcript, receipt, bank or business records. **(Note:** Underlying writing is usually hearsay.)

WRITING DEFINED – Includes all forms of tangible writings, sound and electronic recordings of all forms, and photographs of all sorts including pictures, prints, x-rays, video tapes, and motion pictures. FRE 1001(1)(2).

(2) ORIGINAL – Includes (1) the writing, recording, or photograph itself; (2) any "counterpart" of the original intended to have the same effect as the original (e.g., multiple copies of a contract); (3) any "duplicate original" produced by the same impression as the original (e.g., carbon copies), or from the same plate or matrix (e.g., printed or mimeog'aphed copies), or by photographic process (includes photocopies, enlargements and miniatures). FRE 1001(3)(4). Duplicates are treated as original unless there is a *genuine question of authenticity,* or under the circumstances, the court believes it would be *unfair* not to require the original itself. FRE 1003. Common law does *not* treat photocopies as originals unless they were made in the ordinary course of business as a business record.

(continued)

5. MINIMAL RELIABILITY *(continued)*

(3) PRODUCED – Original need not be actually offered in evidence so long as it is produced for examination and inspection. **Example:** memo qualifying for past recollection recorded may be read into evidence, but writing itself cannot be introduced; same for portions of learned treatises used to cross-examine an expert.

(4) UNAVAILABILITY

– The BER is only a rule of preference; if the original is not available, secondary evidence may be used.

  LOST OR DESTROYED – Sufficient if all originals are lost or destroyed, so long as unavailability does not result from bad faith conduct of proponent. FRE (1004(1).

  UNOBTAINABLE – Cannot be obtained by any available judicial process or procedure. FRE 1004(2).

  POSSESSION OF OPPONENT – Party now objecting was put on notice that the contents of a writing would be in issue at the time he had possession of the original of the writing and said party does not produce the original. FRE 1004(3).

  IMPRACTICALITY – If contents of *voluminous writings* cannot conveniently be examined in court, a chart, summary, or calculation may be presented so long as originals were reasonably made available for inspection and copying. FRE 1006. Also, certified copies of *public records* are admissible because original is "unavailable." FRE 1005.

(5) BURDEN ON PROPONENT – Foundational facts relating to admissibility of secondary evidence (e.g., unavailability) are to be decided by the judge. However, if there is a dispute as to (1) whether the asserted writing ever existed at all; (2) which of several writings is in fact the original; or (3) whether the secondary evidence correctly reflects the contents of the original; the issue is for the jury to decide. FRE 1008. If original is unavailable, any form of secondary evidence is admissible; there is no hierarchy of secondary evidence. Some states prefer written copies to oral testimony.

(6) COLLATERAL ISSUE EXCEPTION – BER does not apply where the writing is not closely related to a controlling issue (i.e., *de minimus* exception). FRE 1004(4).

6. OPINIONS

PERSONAL PERCEPTION – knowledge required by opinion must be *rationally derived* from *personal perception*.

Adequate Opportunity to Perceive – perception must be *sufficient in time and scope* to justify conclusion (look out for split second judgments and perception – impeding facts).

Exceptions – personal knowledge *not* required for (1) opinions of sanity by a *subscribing witness* or (2) opinions about oneself including property, condition mental state, etc. (see below).

Opinions About Oneself – relating to one's own *mental state* (including intent, motive, emotion), *physical or mental condition* (including nature and cause of condition, disease or illness), *personal history* (including name, age, parentage), *property* (including ownership and value), and *value of services*.

Sensory Descriptions – *odors and sounds* and their sources, *colors, temperature, taste.*

Measurements – *speed, weight, height, distances* in general (e.g., "fast," "heavy," "tall," "far,") or specific terms (e.g., mph, pounds, feet and inches).

Identifications – of *property* or *persons* including distinguishing characteristics such as voice, footsteps, age.

Physical Condition of Others – general perceptions of *injury, fatigue, intoxication.*

Mental Condition of Others – rationality, normality, competency and sanity, but stronger foundation of knowledge is required and opinion must avoid legal conclusion.

Meaning of Conduct – "nodding" affirmatively, "indicating" agreement, who "started" or "provoked" a fight. Broad discretion to *exclude* opinions of this type.

NON-EXPERT

SPECIAL NEED – opinion must be *necessary* to *effective communication* of the perception or specially *helpful to a clear understanding of the facts.*

RANGE OF COMMON EXPERIENCE – opinion must be about a *matter* within common experience and within the *scope and range* of common experience. Look out for conclusions re: extreme or refined observations (e.g., 100 mph, 500 yards, 10 tons, explicit diagnoses). If opinion is beyond scope of common experience, must qualify as an expert opinion.

(continued)

6. OPINIONS *(continued)*

EXPERT

BEYOND COMMON EXPERIENCE – opinion must relate to matter that is *sufficiently beyond common experience* so that the opinion of an expert would *assist the trier of fact.* This is especially important when the expert does not have personal knowledge.

QUALIFIED AS AN EXPERT – proponent of expert must persuade the judge that person has special knowledge, skill, experience, training, *or* education to qualify him/her as an expert on the subject to which the opinion relates. Court has broad discretion in this area and each opinion must be measured against the particular qualifications of the witness and the state of the art of the field to which the opinion relates.

Proper Matter – may be based on matters which are not in evidence and which are themselves inadmissible *if* of a type reasonably relied on by experts in the field involved.

If Based on Statement of Another – declarant of statement or opinion providing basis of expert opinion may be called by adverse party and examined as if on cross-X.

If Based on Improper Matter – court must exclude opinion.

Assumed Facts – may be hypothetical in nature and based on explicitly designated "assumed facts" which have been or will be supported by sufficient admissible evidence to sustain a finding of their existence.

Basis of Opinion – expert may but, unless otherwise required by the court, need not state the reasons for the opinion on direct exam. Such reasons may be elicited on cross exam.

BASIS OF OPINION – expert opinion may be based on any proper matter including materials not in evidence, and assumed facts.

Federal Rule – FRE 803(18) provides that expert may be examined re: statements contained in *published* treatises, periodicals, or pamphlets if shown to be *reliable authority* by admission of the witness, other expert testimony or judicial notice. Statements so used are also admissible substantively as an exception to the hearsay rule.

Common Law Rule – expert may *not* be examined in regard to the content or tenor of a published work *unless* (1) the witness referred to, considered or relied upon such publication in arriving at or forming his opinion, (2) the witness wrote the publication, or (3) the publication, has been separately admitted in evidence. If use of statements in a publication are permitted under (1), such statements are *not* admissible as substantive evidence.

CROSS EXAMINATION OF EXPERT – expert may be examined as to (1) qualifications as an expert, (2) subject to which opinion relates, (3) matter and reasons upon which opinion is based, and (4) compensation and any other facts bearing on possible bias.

7. COMMUNICATIONS PRIVILEGES

ISSUE SPOTTING SEQUENCE: (1) *Is there a protected relationship?:* (2) *Was there a communication?* (3) *Was it confidential?* (4) *Has the holder asserted the privilege?* (5) *Was there a waiver?* (6) *Do any exceptions apply?*

(1) RELATIONSHIP — privileges are designed to foster socially important relationships which require mutual trust and confidence; must normally be specified by statute, though FRE applies "common law" to federal cases and state law where state law controls controversy.

INTENT OF COMMUNICATION
– existence of "relationship" determined by the subjective intent of the communicator to derive benefits of protected relationship.

ACTUAL STATUS OF CONFIDANT
– parties must actually be capable of entering privileged relationship; if there is a mistake as to the capacity of a confidant, no privilege (modern view is contra if belief was reasonable).

Client – must seek professional advice or consultation; no prior relationship, actual or anticipated compensation, or actual acceptance of case is required. Corporation is a client if communication is made by an officer or director (i.e., "control group"), *or* by an employee at the direction of a superior.

Patient – must seek diagnosis or treatment; no prior relationship, compensation, or actual treatment required.

Penitent – one who communicates to a clergyperson in accordance with the rules or practice of a religious denomination.

Attorney – must be *licensed to practice law in any state or nation; not* disbarred lawyers and unlicensed law graduates.

Physician – must be *licensed medical practitioner* (M.D. or equivalent) *in any state or nation.*

Psychotherapist – if not an M.D. (*psychiatrists are M.D.'s*) must be licensed under authority of state; some states include marriage counselors, clinical social workers, and psychologists.

Spouse – must be legally married.

Clergy – person must be authorized under rules of the religion to hear confessions.

(2) COMMUNICATION – under common law, only *verbal* communications may be privileged; observations and impressions resulting from confidential protected relationships are *not* protected.

BOTH WAYS – all confidential communications are protected regardless of which party makes them (e.g., attorney's to client/client's to attorney).

GENERATED DURING AND FOR THE RELATIONSHIP – statements, records, and other documents *preexisting* the relationship as well as communications made *incidental* to the relationship are *not* protected even if later transmitted to privileged person, though the "information" may not be elicited from the privileged professional.

MODERN TREND – observations made by a spouse (especially in context of the "marital home") and observations of a medical doctor during physical examination may be protected *if the holder appeared to rely on the sanctity of relationship to permit the observation.*

(continued)

7. COMMUNICATION PRIVILEGES *(continued)*

(3) CONFIDENTIALITY

– communication must be the unique product of the confidential relationship made under circumstances safeguarding the confidentiality; presence of an *inessential person* or a *non-privileged third person* prevents privilege. Confidentiality is presumed; proponent must show no confidentiality.

INESSENTIAL THIRD PERSONS – person is "inessential" unless presence advances the purposes of the relationship (stenographers, researchers, investigators, interpreters, and experts needed by a lawyer are essential.)

NON-PRIVILEGED PERSON – disclosure in the presence of an inessential person does not defeat the privilege if that person is separately privileged (e.g., a spouse).

PROTECTS COMMUNICATION, NOT INFORMATION – even if holder has disclosed the same information in non-privileged contexts, the specific "communication" of that information made in a privileged relationship *is* protected (e.g., lawyer may not be required to testify even if any other person could be).

EAVESDROPPERS – at common law, eavesdroppers may testify (modern view is *contra*) but the communication is still privileged with respect to those in the protected relationship.

(4) HOLDER – the "holder"

controls the privilege; it must be asserted (or waived) by him or on his behalf.

ATTORNEY-CLIENT – client is holder; after death, passes to personal representative.

PHYSICIAN OR PSYCHOTHERAPIST-PATIENT – patient is holder; after death, passes to personal representative.

HUSBAND-WIFE – both parties are holders (even after marriage is dissolved).

CLERGY-PENITENT – usually both are holders.

JUDGE MAY ASSERT – in the absence of a holder or authorized representative, the court may, on its own motion, assert privilege.

(5) WAIVER – privilege is waived if holder (1) *voluntarily reveals a significant part of the communication,* or (2) *fails to object to disclosure when he had an opportunity and right to do so.*

(6) EXCEPTIONS – for public

policy reasons, privileges may not be asserted in certain situations, especially where the lawsuit is between the parties to the privileged relationship or to joint holders of the same privilege.

ATTORNEY-CLIENT – privilege not applicable (1) in suit between attorney and client, (2) in suit between joint clients, (3) where communication was designed to advance a crime or fraud, or (4) if the communication relates to the intent of a now deceased client with respect to the disposition of property.

PHYSICIAN OR PSYCHOTHERAPIST-PATIENT – privilege not applicable (1) in suit between doctor and patient, (2) patient has put his mental or physical condition in issue, (3) doctor appointed by court, or (4) in criminal cases (minority view – e.g., California).

HUSBAND-WIFE – not applicable (1) in suit between holders, or (2) in criminal case based on assault of spouse or child.

CLERGY-PENITENT – no exceptions; applicable in all actions.

KAPLAN) *pmbr*

ISSUE SPOTTING SEQUENCE: *(1) Is there an assertion? (2) Was it made out of court? (3) Who is the declarant? (4) What is asserted?*

(1) ASSERTION

    VERBAL COMMUNICATION – includes all written and oral assertions, including tape recordings.

    NON-VERBAL COMMUNICATION

        ASSERTIVE CONDUCT – gesture or act done with the *primary intent* to assert or communicate information or opinion (e.g., lineup I.D., "o.k." sign); usually in response to a question.

        NON-ASSERTIVE CONDUCT – under some theories of hearsay (*not* the FRE), conduct is treated as an assertion if the act is used as *circumstantial evidence of the belief of the actor* in order to *prove the truth of the belief* – the conduct is used as an implied assertion of belief (e.g., the fact that a ship captain took his family aboard a ship used to prove the ship was seaworthy).

(2) OUT-OF-COURT – any assertion not made at the present hearing, *including* assertions made in other courts, assertions made under oath, and all writings.

(3) DECLARANT – person who made the out-of-court assertion; the source of the information (identification of the declarant is critical to analysis of the "assertion" and the substantive assertion contained therein).

(4) ASSERTION – isolate the statement made by the declarant (as opposed to the "testimony" of the witness reporting the statement) to determine precisely what is being asserted. **Note:** If there are two or more out-of-court statements (e.g., a written report of an oral statement), analyze each assertion separately.

8. APPROACH TO HEARSAY *(continued)*

ISSUE SPOTTING SEQUENCE: *(5) Is the assertion relevant for a non-hearsay use (i.e., a use not dependent on the statement's truth)? (6) If used to prove its truth, is the assertion specifically exempted from the hearsay rule? (7) If neither an exclusion nor an exemption apply, does the assertion qualify for a hearsay exception?*

(5) RELEVANT NON-HEARSAY USE (HEARSAY EXCLUSIONS) – under the definition of hearsay, an out-of-court assertion is hearsay only if it is offered to prove its truth. If the evidentiary value of a statement is not dependent on the accuracy of the assertion contained therein, the reliability of the declarant is not critical, and the need for cross-examination is removed. Out-of-court assertions relevant irrespective of their truth are non-hearsay (i.e., they are *excluded* from the hearsay rule).

STATE OF MIND – fact that statement was made tends to prove a *relevant state of mind of the declarant or listener irrespective of the truth of the assertion (normally, used to prove knowledge, intent, attitude, or belief of a party).*

IMPEACHMENT OR REHABILITATION – prior statement of a witness used to impeach or rehabilitate (prior statement need not be true to show inconsistency nor to rebut charge of recent fabrication). **Note:** FRE permits sworn statements made at a hearing or deposition to be used as substantive evidence.

VERBAL EVENT – statement which has probative significance totally independent of any communicative content: (1) *transactional words* (e.g., contract or a will, operative words of a legal notice, demand, or donative intent, (2) *tortious words* of defamation, and (3) *questions or commands*, etc.

(6) STATUTORY EXEMPTIONS – FRE 801(d) specifically *exempts* from the hearsay definition certain kinds of out-of-court statements even *though they are offered to prove their truth and* otherwise meet the hearsay definition.

ADMISSIONS (see Hearsay Exception Flowchart 10) – though treated as non-hearsay under the FRE, the nature and scope of "admissions" are analyzed in the more traditional context of hearsay *exceptions*. FRE 801(d)(2).

PRIOR IDENTIFICATIONS – *if declarant testifies in court* with respect to identification of a person, any prior statement identifying the person made after perceiving him is non-hearsay. FRE 801(d)(1)(c).

PRIOR CONSISTENT STATEMENTS – *if declarant testifies* and has been *impeached by a claim of recent fabrication or undue influence*, any statement made prior to the alleged time of fabrication or undue influence is non-hearsay. FRE 801(d)(1)(B).

PRIOR SWORN INCONSISTENT STATEMENTS – *if declarant testifies*, any prior *sworn* statement (subject to penalty of perjury) is non-hearsay if given at trial, hearing, or deposition. FRE 801(d)(1)(A).

(7) ADMISSIBLE HEARSAY (EXCEPTIONS) – if an out-of-court assertion *is* offered to prove its truth and it is not exempted by the FRE, it is hearsay. Much hearsay, however, is admitted because of considerations of trustworthiness, necessity, and fairness. The scope and form of admissible hearsay is embodied in the 30 or so *hearsay exceptions* enumerated in FRE 803 and 804. The most important exceptions are analyzed in Flowchart 10.

9. HEARSAY EXCEPTIONS AND EXEMPTIONS

ADMISSIONS
DIRECT ADMISSION – (1) statement of a party (2) offered against that party.

ADOPTIVE – (1) statement made in party's presence (2) party's conduct or silence manifests adoption of truth (3) offered against that party.

AUTHORIZED – (1) declarant authorized by party (2) to speak concerning the subject (3) offered against the authorizing party.

EMPLOYEE/AGENT (FRE, not Common Law) – (1) statement by a party's employee or agent (2) made during the relationship (3) concerning a matter within the scope of employment (4) offered against the party.

CO-CONSPIRATOR – (1) statement by a co-conspirator of party (2) made in furtherance of the conspiratorial goal (3) offered against: the party (4) if independent evidence of conspiracy (5) sufficient to persuade judge (common law contra-prima facie case sufficient).

DECLARATION AGAINST INTEREST
(1) unavailable declarant (includes death, incompetency, beyond jurisdiction, assertion of privilege)
(2) against financial or penal interest (common law – financial only)
(3) against interest when made
(4) reasonable person would not make it unless true

DYING DECLARATION
(1) unavailable declarant (common law – declarant must be dead)
(2) belief that death was imminent
(3) relates to cause or circumstances of threatened death
(4) personal knowledge, not opinion or speculation
(5) offered in civil or criminal homicide case (common law – homicide only)

OFFICIAL WRITTEN STATEMENT
(1) written statement (including electronic data)
(2) by public official
(3) setting forth (a) activities of public office, or (b) observations made or recorded in course of legal duties (*not* police report in criminal case), or (c) factual findings of official investigation (*not* against D in criminal case) unless circumstances indicate lack of trustworthiness.

PAST RECOLLECTION RECORDED
(1) memo or record of facts
(2) personal knowledge of declarant or reliable source
(3) made when facts were fresh
(4) memory exhausted
(5) declarant testifies it accurately reflects former knowledge
(6) may be read into evidence only (unless adverse party offers)

PRIOR TESTIMONY
(1) testimony given under oath
(2) previously given in former hearing or deposition
(3) party (or predecessor in interest) *against* whom offered
(4) had *opportunity* and *similar incentive* examine testimony (common law – parties and issues must be identical)
(5) unavailable declarant (prosecutor has special heavy burden)

SENSE IMPRESSION (FRE, not Common Law)
(1) statement describing or explaining an event or condition
(2) made while or immediately after declarant was perceiving it

(continued)

9. HEARSAY EXCEPTIONS AND EXEMPTIONS *(continued)*

EXCITED UTTERANCE
(1) startling event
(2) made under stress of excitement (common law – statement must be spontaneous, and made during or immediately after event)
(3) relating to event

MENTAL STATE
PRESENT MENTAL STATE – explicit statement of mental state may prove existence of the mental state or conduct of declarant consistent with intent (some courts allow to prove conduct of a third person)
FORMER MENTAL STATE – explicit statement of past belief or remembrance may prove facts re declarant's will, but not otherwise.

PHYSICAL STATE
PRESENT PHYSICAL STATE – description of present sensation or condition may prove existence of condition (need not be made to a doctor).
FORMER PHYSICAL STATE (FRE, not Common Law) – (1) statement or description of (a) medical history, or (b) past symptom or sensation, or (c) character or nature of external cause (2) *if made for diagnosis or treatment* (3) and *if pertinent* to diagnosis or treatment.

BUSINESS RECORD
(1) written statement (including electronic data)
(2) made in regular course of business
(3) near time of receipt of information
(4) declarant has personal knowledge or source reliable
(5) unless circumstances indicate lack of trustworthiness

EXPERT CROSS-EXAMINATION (FRE, not Common Law)
(1) during examination of expert
(2) statements in treatises, periodicals or pamphlets
(3) established as reliable authority by (a) testimony, (b) admission of witness, or (c) judicial notice
(4) may be read into evidence (not admissible as exhibit)

EQUIVALENCY (FRE, not Common Law)
(1) circumstantial guarantees of trustworthiness equivalent to other exceptions
(2) evidence of a material fact
(3) more probative than other reasonably available evidence
(4) interests of justice will be served
(5) timely notice to adverse party providing fair opportunity to response (including particulars of statement, name and address of declarant)

IDENTIFICATION (FRE, not Common Law)
(1) prior statement of a witness-declarant
(2) identifying a person
(3) made after perceiving that person

CONSISTENT STATEMENT (FRE, not Common Law)
(1) prior statement of a witness-declarant
(2) consistent with testimony
(3) offered to rebut charge of recent fabrication or improper influence or motive

INCONSISTENT STATEMENT (FRE, not Common Law)
(1) prior statement of a witness
(2) inconsistent with testimony
(3) given subject to penalty of perjury
(4) at a deposition, trial, or other proceeding

ADDEM P. BOPP, SEE ICI

10. THE BIG 10 EXCEPTIONS

A-Admission **D-**Declaration v. Interest **D-**Dying Declaration **E-**Excited Utterance **M-**Mental State **P-**Physical State **B-**Business Record
O-Official Records **P-**Past Recollection Recorded **P-**Prior Recorded Testimony

STATEMENTS OF PARTY-OPPONENT – (1) statement *made by a party* to a lawsuit (2) *offered against him* by his opponent. Personal knowledge of declarant *not* required; need *not* be against interest when made; includes pleas of guilty (unless withdrawn); but not convictions. FRE 801(d)(2)(A).

STATEMENT ADOPTED BY PARTY-OPPONENT (TACIT ADMISSION)
– (1) statement *of another* (2) *made to or in the presence of a party* (3) *who by conduct or silence manifests an unequivocal adoption or belief* in the truth of the statement, and (4) *offered against the party* by his opponent. FRE 801(d)(2)0B).

A-ADMISSION – Rationale:
gamesmanship and fairness – a party should not be permitted to exclude his own statements because of inability to cross-examine. Treated as non-hearsay *exemption* under FRE; a hearsay *exception* under common law.

STATEMENT OF ANOTHER ATTRIBUTED TO PARTY-OPPONENT (VICARIOUS ADMISSION) – (1) statement *made by another* (2) *attributed to a party* and (3) *offered against the party* by his opponent.

Must Hear and Be Able To Deny – party must have heard or read statement, and he must have been reasonably capable of denying truth of assertion.

Reasonable To Expect Denial – circumstances must have been such that a reasonable person would have denied the assertion if it were not true; remember right to silence in custodial situations.

Authorized Statements – (1) a statement made by a person explicitly or implicitly *authorized by a party* (2) *to speak on the party's behalf* (3) *offered against the party* by his opponent. Authority to speak is not necessarily co-extensive with authority to act. FRE 801(d)(2)(C).

Employee Statements – (1) a statement *made by a party's employee or agent* (2) *concerning a matter within the scope of his agency or employment* (3) made during the course of the relationship (4) *offered against the party* by his opponent. No authority to speak is required; common law has no similar provision. FRE 801(d)(2)(D).

Statement of Co-Conspirator – (1) a statement *made by a party's co-conspirator* (2) *during the conspiracy* and (3) *in furtherance of the conspiratorial goal* (4) *offered against the party* by the prosecutor (5) if the underlying conspiracy can be established by independent evidence sufficient to persuade the judge (by preponderance) that conspiracy exists. FRE 801(d)(2)(E). Common law only requires *prima facie* case prior to admission, not preponderance.

Statement of Predecessor in Interest – (1) statement made by a previous owner of property (2) during ownership (3) offered against the owner-party by his opponent. Common law, *not* FRE.

Statement of Decedent in a Wrongful Death Action –
(1) statements made by the decedent in a wrongful death action (2) offered against the party who brings the action. Common law, *not* FRE.

(continued)

10. THE BIG 10 EXCEPTIONS *(continued)*

D-DECLARATION AGAINST INTEREST – (1) statement by an *unavailable declarant* (2) so far *against financial or penal interests* (3) *when made (4) that a reasonable person would not have made it unless he believed it to be true.* FRE 804(b)(3). **Rationale:** unavailability indicates necessity, against interest assures trustworthiness. If statement is against penal interest and is offered to exculpate D, "corroborating circumstances must clearly indicate trustworthiness." Common law limits statements to those against financial interest; a small minority admit statements against social interest as well.

D-DYING DECLARATION – (1) statement by an *unavailable declarant* (2) made while the *declarant believed his death was imminent* (3) concerning the *cause or circumstances* of what he believed to be his impending death which is (4) offered in a *homicide prosecution or any civil case.* FRE 804 (b)(2). **Rationale:** declarant would not want to die with a lie on his lips.

INADMISSIBLE IN CRIMINAL CASES OTHER THAN HOMICIDE – common law *only* admits in criminal homicide cases; FRE extends to civil cases, but not other types of criminal cases.

DECLARANT NEED NOT BE DEAD – (common law is contra).

PERSONAL KNOWLEDGE – statement must relate personal observations not opinion or speculation.

E-EXCITED UTTERANCE – (1) statement *relating to a* (2) *startling event* or condition (3) made while the *declarant was under the stress.* FRE 803(2). **Rationale:** excitement and stress preclude fabrication.

SPONTANEITY NOT REQUIRED – under strict common law rule, statement must be "spontaneous" (the intervention of a question such as "What happened?" can defeat exception, and creates opportunity for fabrication), not so in FRE.

TIMING OF STATEMENT – under common law, statement must be made "during or immediately after the exciting event." Under FRE, substantial time may pass so long as declarant is still under original stress of the event.

DECLARANT – need not be known or identified; availability is of no consequence.

M-MENTAL STATE – statements which purport to *directly and explicitly* state or describe declarant's mental or emotional condition. FRE 803(3). Distinguish from statements which are merely *circumstantial evidence* of the declarant's state of mind (i.e., hearsay exclusions).

PRESENT MENTAL STATE – *statement purporting to reveal any presently held intent, belief, attitude, emotion, or feeling is admissible to prove the true existence of that mental state.* Some states allow statement to prove conduct of person other than declarant, but FRE comment urges contrary construction. **Rationale:** no memory or perception problems.

FORMER MENTAL STATE – *statement of memory or belief is not admissible to prove the fact remembered or believed unless it relates to relevant facts concerning the declarant's will.* **Rationale:** expediency and necessity.

P-PHYSICAL STATE – statements which purport to state or describe declarant's physical sensations or condition.

PRESENT PHYSICAL STATE – *statement purporting to describe any present physical sensation or condition is admissible to prove the existence of that physical state.* Includes statements of present pain made to any person. FRE 803(3). **Rationale:** no memory or perception problems: tends to be necessary.

FORMER PHYSICAL STATE – (1) statement purporting to describe a medical history including *past pain, symptom or sensation, or the inception or general character of the external source of the physical condition is admissible if:* (2)*it was made for purposes of medical diagnosis or treatment, and* (3) it is *reasonably pertinent to the diagnosis or treatment.* FRE 803(4). **Rationale:** no perception problems, desire for effective diagnosis or treatment tends to guarantee sincerity and trustworthiness.

10. THE BIG 10 EXCEPTIONS *(continued)*

B-BUSINESS RECORD

– (1) *written statement* (2) *made in the regular course of business* (3) *at or near the time of receipt of the information* (4) *by a person with knowledge* (5) *unless the source of the information or circumstances of preparation indicate lack of trustworthiness.* FRE 803(6). **Rationale:** memory problems are avoided by requirement of timely recording and trustworthiness is assured by systematic checking, continuity and business reliance on the statements.

FOUNDATION – foundation may be established by the custodian of the record or any person who can identify the record and testify as to mode of preparation; the declarant need not testify.

DATA COMPILATION – business records may be in the form of electric data storage tapes and the like.

OPINIONS OR DIAGNOSIS – statement may contain an *opinion or diagnosis*. Common law is generally contra.

KNOWLEDGE – declarant must have personal knowledge or information recorded *or* the record must be made from information transmitted by one with knowledge.

BUSINESS – "business" includes any institution (including the government), association, profession or occupation.

REGULAR COURSE OF BUSINESS – many cases exclude records made for purposes of litigation (even if made by an investigator in the regular course of his duties); FRE has no absolute rule, but authorizes the court to exclude records where there is a manifest lack of trustworthiness.

ABSENCE OF ENTRY – (1) evidence that a matter is *not* included in a business record is (2) *admissible to prove the non-occurrence or non-existence of the matter if the matter was of a kind that was regularly reported* unless the sources of information or other circumstances indicate a *lack of trustworthiness*. FRE 803(7).

COMMERCIAL PUBLICATIONS – (1) statement contained in *market quotations, tabulations, lists, directories, or other published compilations* (2) *generally used and relied upon* (3) by the public or persons in particular occupations. FRE 803(17).

(continued)

10. THE BIG 10 EXCEPTIONS *(continued)*

O-OFFICIAL WRITTEN STATEMENTS (Public Records) – Rationale: special trustworthiness is derived from fact that statement was made by or to a public employee with duty to accurately record and no apparent motive to falsify: necessity results from likelihood that declarant will have no independent memory of contents. "Record" includes reports, statements, or data compilations (including electronic data) in any form.

RECORD OF PUBLIC ACTIVITY – (1) *written statement* (2) *of a public employee or agency* (3) *concerning the activities of the public office or agency.* FRE 803(8)(A).

RECORD OF OBSERVATION – (1) *written statement* (2) *of a public employee or agency* (3) *concerning observations made* (4) *while carrying out a duty imposed by law* (5) *as to matters which there was a duty to report* (6) *except that in criminal cases, records of observations made by law officers are not admissible.* FRE 803(8)(B).

REPORT OF FINDINGS – (1) *written statement* (2) *of a public officer or agency of factual findings or conclusions* (3) *resulting from an investigation or inquiry within the employee's or agency's legal duties* (4) *unless the sources of information or other circumstances indicate a lack of trustworthiness* (5) *except that such reports are not admissible against a criminal defendant.* FRE 803(8)(C).

ABSENCE OF RECORD OR ENTRY – (1) *evidence that a matter is not included in a public record is* (2) *admissible to prove the non-occurrence or non-existence of a matter of which record is regularly made and preserved* (3) *if a certification is offered, or if testimony is produced to show that a diligent search failed to disclose the record or entry.* FRE 803(10).

RECORDS OF VITAL STATISTICS – (1) *written statements* (2) *of births, fetal deaths, deaths or marriages if* (3) *the report was made to a public official* (4) *pursuant to requirements of law.* FRE 803(9).

CERTIFICATE OF MARRIAGE, BAPTISM AND SIMILAR – (1) *written certificate* (2) *issued by a clergyman, public official or other person* (3) *authorized by law or the practices of a religion to perform a marriage or religious ceremony* (4) *indicating that such ceremony was performed* (5) *if the certificate was issued at the time of the act or within a reasonable time thereafter.* FRE 803(12).

RECORDS OF DOCUMENTS AFFECTING PROPERTY – (1) *record of public office* (2) *relating to the existence, content, execution or delivery of a document* (3) *which affects an interest in property (not just land) if* (4) *such record is kept pursuant to statutory authority.* FRE 803(14). May prove content of document as well as fact of execution or delivery.

(continued)

10. THE BIG 10 EXCEPTIONS (continued)

P-PAST RECOLLECTION RECORDED – (1) statement contained in a *memorandum or record* (2) made by one with *personal knowledge* (3) recording facts perceived by him while the *matter was still fresh in the declarant's mind* provided that (4) the *declarant has first exhausted his present recollection*, (5) testified that he knows the *statement truly reflected his knowledge at the time* and (6) the statement *is read into evidence* only. FRE 803(5). **Rationale:** memory problems avoided by requirement of timely record, necessity results from exhausted memory and trustworthiness somewhat safeguarded by opportunity to cross-examine declarant.

⎰ **DECLARANT MUST TESTIFY** – person who wrote memo must testify as a witness to lay necessary foundation re: exhausted present memory and accuracy of memo.

PRESENT MEMORY EXHAUSTED – court must find that declarant-witness has insufficient recollection to enable full and accurate testimony on the fact(s) recorded.

NOT ADMISSIBLE AS EXHIBIT – writing itself not admissible unless offered by the adverse party.

RELATED ISSUES – distinguish from (1) present memory refreshed where memo actually jogs recollection and is not used as substantive evidence; (2) business record where memo made in ordinary course of business; (3) look out for multiple hearsay – look to reliability of the ultimate source of information.

P-PRIOR TESTIMONY – (1) statement made in the form of *testimony* (2) by an *unavailable person* (3) *given at another hearing or in a deposition* (4) if the *party against whom the testimony is now offered* (or his predecessor in interest) (5) had an *opportunity* and (6) *similar motive to develop the testimony* on direct or cross-examination. FRE 804(b)(1). **Rationale:** necessity is a result of unavailability and trustworthiness is supported by prior opportunity to develop and examine testimony.

⎰ **TESTIMONY** – must be under oath or affirmation, but need not be recorded in verbatim transcript (even if it is, the transcript is not required).

UNAVAILABILITY – in criminal cases, prosecutor must show every reasonable and diligent effort to produce declarant.

SIMILAR ISSUES – issues need not be identical (common law was contra) and testimony may be given in unrelated proceeding if the *present opponent* was involved in suit and had opportunity and incentive to develop testimony.

SIMILAR PARTIES – parties need not be identical (common law contra); person offering testimony need not have been involved in prior proceeding; in civil cases, party must accept testimony previously offered by or against predecessor in interest.

11. EXAMINATION OF WITNESSES

NARRATIVE – Question too broad and general; testimony will be less rapid, distinct or effective than is reasonably possible and tends to include irrelevant and other inadmissible responses.

LEADING – Question on *direct exam* suggests the desired response by its form, substance or tone. Leading questions *are allowed*: (1) on *cross-exam*; (2) as to *undisputed preliminary facts*; (3) in examining witnesses with *comprehensive problems*; (4) in examining *hostile witnesses on direct*; (5) in examining *experts*; (6) when used to *refresh recollection*.

ARGUMENTATIVE – Question not asked for purpose of eliciting new information but for rhetorical or argumentative effect.

ASSUMING FACTS NOT IN EVIDENCE – Question contains an assumption of a fact that is not supported by any evidence in the record (e.g., "Are you still beating your dog?").

COMPOUND – Question embodies at least two separate aspects which make the answer unclear or ambiguous. Look for questions containing "or" as well as separate questions attached by "and" (e.g., "Did you see *or* hear him come home?" "Did you see *and* hear come home?").

AMBIGUOUS OR UNINTELLIGIBLE – Question that is unclear as to meaning or that may not be easily understood by the witness or invites an answer that may not be easily understood in light of the question.

OBJECTIONS TO FORM

SPECULATION – Question asks witness to speculate or conjecture (aspect of opinion testimony). Look out for "Is it possible" questions. Witness need not be certain but must be able to answer with a reasonable degree of conviction.

ASKED AND ANSWERED – Question previously answered adequately resulting in unconstructive repetition and cumulative evidence – broad leeway allowed on cross-exam.

MISSTATES EVIDENCE – Question contains preface which misstates, characterizes or misconstrues evidence or testimony.

OPPRESSIVE AND HARASSING – Question or conduct which will cause witness undue embarrassment or emotional stress.

NON-RESPONSIVE – Answer is not responsive to Question; either party may have answer stricken. Court has discretion to not strike unresponsive answers and volunteered testimony if it is otherwise relevant and admissible, and if elicited by a proper question.

1. FREEHOLD ESTATES

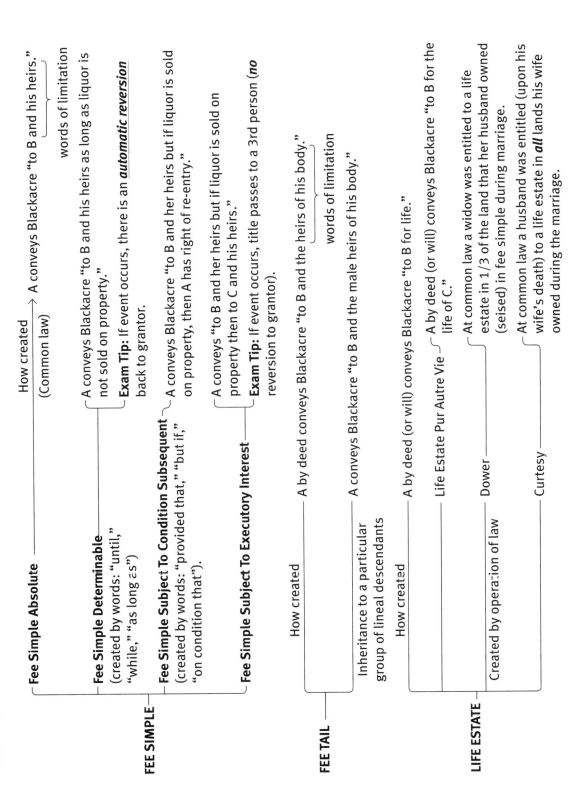

FEE SIMPLE

Fee Simple Absolute

How created

(Common law) → A conveys Blackacre "to B and his heirs."

words of limitation

Fee Simple Determinable
(created by words: "until," "while," "as long as")

A conveys Blackacre "to B and his heirs as long as liquor is not sold on property."

words of limitation — *automatic reversion*

Exam Tip: If event occurs, there is an *automatic reversion* back to grantor.

Fee Simple Subject To Condition Subsequent
(created by words: "provided that," "but if," "on condition that").

A conveys Blackacre "to B and her heirs but if liquor is sold on property, then A has right of re-entry."

Fee Simple Subject To Executory Interest

A conveys "to B and her heirs but if liquor is sold on property then to C and his heirs."

Exam Tip: If event occurs, title passes to a 3rd person (*no* reversion to grantor).

FEE TAIL

How created

A by deed conveys Blackacre "to B and the heirs of his body."

words of limitation

A conveys Blackacre "to B and the male heirs of his body."

Inheritance to a particular group of lineal descendants

LIFE ESTATE

How created

A by deed (or will) conveys Blackacre "to B for life."

Life Estate Pur Autre Vie — A by deed (or will) conveys Blackacre "to B for the life of C."

Created by operation of law

Dower — At common law a widow was entitled to a life estate in 1/3 of the land that her husband owned (seised) in fee simple during marriage.

Curtesy — At common law a husband was entitled (upon his wife's death) to a life estate in *all* lands his wife owned during the marriage.

2. NON-FREEHOLD ESTATES

ESTATE FOR YEARS

How created: L leases Blackacre to T for the period January 1, 1992 to December 31, 1994 (a period of 3 years).

Characteristics:
- Specific time for beginning and ending
- Ends automatically
- Subject to statute of frauds

PERIODIC TENANCY
also referred to as ESTATE FROM YEAR TO YEAR

How created: L leases Blackacre to T "from month to month" (or year to year).

Characteristics:
- No specific termination date
- Automatically renews
- Notice is required for termination

TENANCY AT WILL

How created: L leases Blackacre to T for "as long as L wishes."

Characteristics:
- Either party may terminate at will.
- No notice is required.
- Terminates by operation of law:
  (1) either party dies;
  (2) tenant commits waste; or
  (3) landlord sells property.

TENANCY AT SUFFERANCE
(Hold-over Tenant)

T **wrongfully** remains in possession of premises **after** the expiration of a lawful tenancy.

Landlord Remedies:
- Eviction
- Creation of periodic tenancy
- Forcible entry, which most states by statute prohibit

3. FUTURE INTERESTS

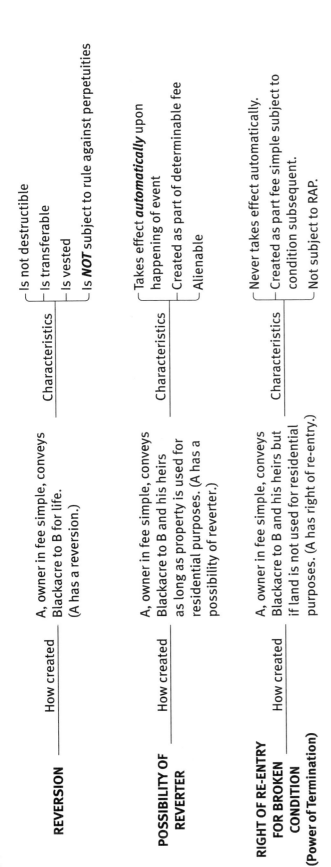

REVERSION —— How created —— A, owner in fee simple, conveys Blackacre to B for life. (A has a reversion.)

Characteristics
- Is not destructible
- Is transferable
- Is vested
- Is **NOT** subject to rule against perpetuities

POSSIBILITY OF REVERTER —— How created —— A, owner in fee simple, conveys Blackacre to B and his heirs as long as property is used for residential purposes. (A has a possibility of reverter.)

Characteristics
- Takes effect **automatically** upon happening of event
- Created as part of determinable fee
- Alienable

RIGHT OF RE-ENTRY FOR BROKEN CONDITION (Power of Termination) —— How created —— A, owner in fee simple, conveys Blackacre to B and his heirs but if land is not used for residential purposes. (A has right of re-entry.)

Characteristics
- Never takes effect automatically.
- Created as part fee simple subject to condition subsequent.
- Not subject to RAP.

(continued)

3. FUTURE INTERESTS *(continued)*

REMAINDERS

Vested

Not subject to RAP

A, owner in fee simple, conveys Blackacre to B for life, remainder to C and his heirs. (C has a vested remainder.)

TYPES

- Absolutely vested
- Vested subject to *partial defeasance*
- Vested subject to total defeasance

  - Must follow natural termination of prior estate
  - Follows a life estate, fee tail or estate for years
  - Cannot follow a fee simple estate

Contingent

A, owner in fee, conveys Blackacre to B for life, remainder to C and his heirs if C pays A $100. (C has a contingent remainder.)

TYPES

- Subject to condition precedent
- Created in favor of an unborn or unascertained person

  - Not destructible (modern view)
  - Are transferable (modern view)
  - Subject to claims of creditors (modern view)
  - Subject to RAP

EXECUTORY INTERESTS

Shifting

A, owner in fee, conveys Blackacre to B for life, but if B marries C, then to C and his heirs. (C has a shifting executory interest.)

Springing

A, owner in fee, devises Blackacre to B and his heirs one year after A's death. (B has a springing executory devise.)

Characteristics

- Cuts short prior estate before its natural termination
- Prior estate may be a fee simple, life estate or fee tail
- Subject to RAP
- Alienable and contingent

4. NON-POSSESSORY INTERESTS IN LAND

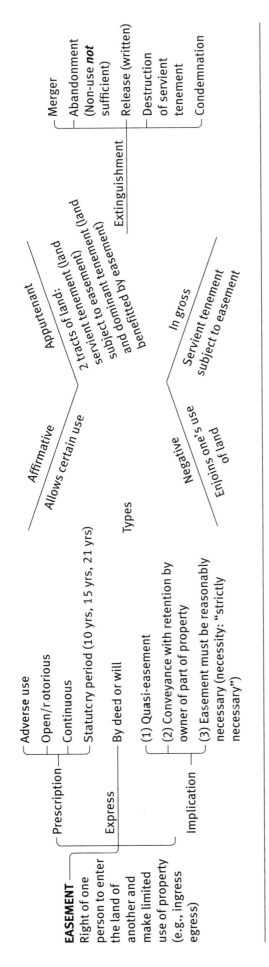

EASEMENT
Right of one person to enter the land of another and make limited use of property (e.g., ingress egress)

Prescription
- Adverse use
- Open/notorious
- Continuous
- Statutory period (10 yrs, 15 yrs, 21 yrs)

Express — By deed or will

Implication
- (1) Quasi-easement
- (2) Conveyance with retention by owner of part of property
- (3) Easement must be reasonably necessary (necessity: "strictly necessary")

Types

Affirmative — Allows certain use

Appurtenant — 2 tracts of land: servient tenement (land subject to easement and dominant tenement benefitted by easement)

In gross — Servient tenement subject to easement

Negative — Enjoins one's use of land

Extinguishment
- Merger
- Abandonment (Non-use *not* sufficient)
- Release (written)
- Destruction of servient tenement
- Condemnation

PROFIT
Right of one person to enter the land of another and extract something therefrom (e.g., crops, sand, oil)

Requires Compliance w/S/F

Types
- Affirmative
- Negative
- Appurtenant
- In gross

Extinguishment
- Merger
- Abandonment
- Release
- Destruction of servient tenement
- Condemnation

(continued)

4. NON-POSSESSORY INTERESTS IN LAND *(continued)*

LICENSE

Permission to enter another's property without being trespasser

- Revocable
- Irrevocable — License Coupled w/Interest
- Characteristics
  - Personal in nature
  - No writing required
  - Permissive use
  - No prescriptive rights

	LICENSE	EASEMENT	CONTRACT
Consideration:	May be required	Not required	Required
S/F:	No writing required	Writing required	Oral/Written
Revocable:	Yes	No	No

COVENANT RUNNING WITH LAND

- **Requirements**
  - Writing
  - Intent
  - Touch & concern land
  - Privity of estate
- **Privity**
  - Horizontal bet. Original Covenanting Parties
  - Vertical — Required to bound successors
- **Remedies for Breach**
  - At law — Money damages
  - Equity — Injunctive relief
  - Extinguishment
    - Merger
    - Release
    - Condemnation
    - Abandonment

EQUITABLE SERVITUDE

- **Requirements**
  - Writing (notice)
  - Intent
  - Touch & concern
  - No privity required
- **Equitable Defenses**
  - Unclean hands
  - Estoppel
  - Changed neighborhood conditions
- **Common scheme**
  - Negative covenants will be implied
  - Notice — Grantor's intent
- **Extinguishment**
  - Merger
  - Release
  - Condemnation
  - Changed neighborhood conditions

5. CONVEYANCING

VENDOR-PURCHASER

- Land sale contract
  - S/F applies
    - exception: part performance doctrine
  - Identify parties
  - Describe land
  - Purchase price
  - Signed by maker
- Equitable conversion
  - Majority view
    - Vendee equitable owner
    - Risk of loss on vendee
- Marketable title
  - at closing

TITLE DEFECTS:
- Mortgage
- Easement
- Tax lien
- Outstanding reverter rights

DEED

- Delivery (grantor's intent)
- Acceptance presumed
- Types
  - Quitclaim (no warranties)
  - Warranty (Contains all 6 covenants)
  - Special warranty (Specified covenants)
- Covenants of title
  - Seisin
  - Right to convey
  - Encumbrancers — Personal in nature—do **not** run w/ land
  - Quiet Enjoyment
  - Warranty
  - Further assurances — Run w/ land
- Estoppel by deed
  - X conveys greater interest in prop. than she owns
  - after-acquired interest inures to grantee
- Minority View

(continued)

5. CONVEYANCING *(continued)*

RECORDING ACTS
(protects purchasers not donees, heirs, or devisees)

Pure Race — ┤ Whoever records first wins
                └ Actual notice irrelevant

Notice — ┤ Subsequent bfp prevails
             └ Bfp need not record

Race-notice — ┤ Subsequent bfp prevails
                  └ Bfp must also record *first*

MORTGAGES
(Security interest in land)

Types — ┤ Lien theory
            └ Title theory
              Transfer legal title to mortgagee

Redemption
(generally mortgagor has redemp rt.)

┤ Equity: mortgagor can pay off mortgage prior to foreclosure
└ Statutory: mortgagor can redeem for some fixed period after foreclosure

PRIORITIES
(Determined by time when mortgage is recorded)

┤ Prior mortgage prevails over subsequent one
├ Unrecorded mortgage not protected
├ If foreclosure proceeds insufficient, deficiency judgment allowed
└ Transfer by mortgagor: grantee who assumes mortgage becomes personally liable

6. CONCURRENT ESTATES

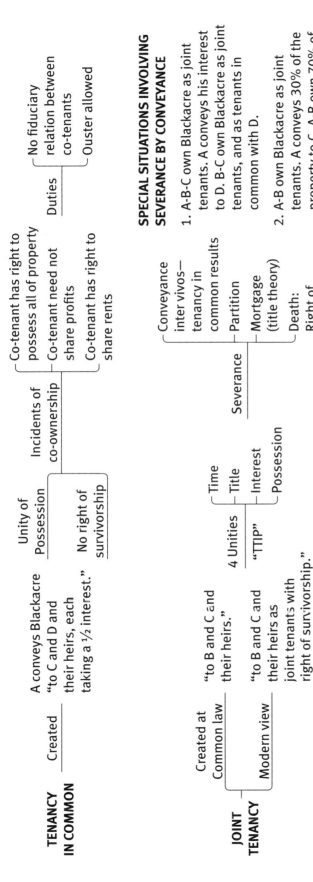

TENANCY IN COMMON

Created — A conveys Blackacre "to C and D and their heirs, each taking a ½ interest."

Incidents of co-ownership
- Co-tenant has right to possess all of property
- Co-tenant need not share profits
- Co-tenant has right to share rents
- Duties
  - No fiduciary relation between co-tenants
  - Ouster allowed

Unity of Possession
- No right of survivorship

JOINT TENANCY

Created at Common law — "to B and C and their heirs."

Modern view — "to B and C and their heirs as joint tenants with right of survivorship."

4 Unities "TTIP"
- Time
- Title
- Interest
- Possession

Severance
- Conveyance inter vivos—tenancy in common results
- Partition
- Mortgage (title theory)
- Death: Right of survivorship

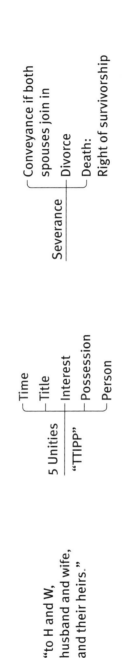

SPECIAL SITUATIONS INVOLVING SEVERANCE BY CONVEYANCE

1. A-B-C own Blackacre as joint tenants. A conveys his interest to D. B-C own Blackacre as joint tenants, and as tenants in common with D.

2. A-B own Blackacre as joint tenants. A conveys 30% of the property to C. A-B own 70% of Blackacre as joint tenants and B-C own 30% as tenants in common.

TENANCY BY THE ENTIRETY

Created — "to H and W, husband and wife, and their heirs."

5 Unities "TTIPP"
- Time
- Title
- Interest
- Possession
- Person

Severance
- Conveyance if both spouses join in
- Divorce
- Death: Right of survivorship

1. INTENTIONAL TORTS: PERSONAL AND EMOTIONAL INJURY

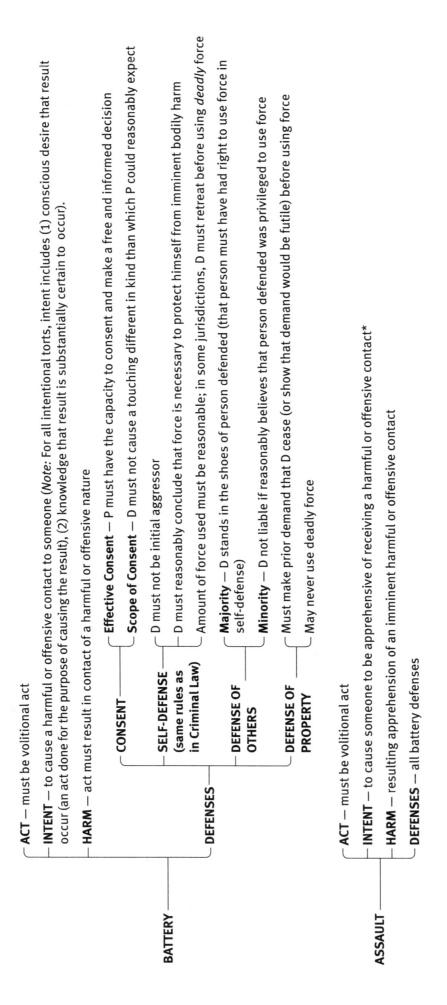

BATTERY

- **ACT** — must be volitional act

- **INTENT** — to cause a harmful or offensive contact to someone (*Note:* For all intentional torts, intent includes (1) conscious desire that result occur (an act done for the purpose of causing the result), (2) knowledge that result is substantially certain to occur).

- **HARM** — act must result in contact of a harmful or offensive nature

- **DEFENSES**
  - **CONSENT**
    - **Effective Consent** — P must have the capacity to consent and make a free and informed decision
    - **Scope of Consent** — D must not cause a touching different in kind than which P could reasonably expect
  - **SELF-DEFENSE (same rules as in Criminal Law)**
    - D must not be initial aggressor
    - D must reasonably conclude that force is necessary to protect himself from imminent bodily harm
    - Amount of force used must be reasonable; in some jurisdictions, D must retreat before using *deadly* force
  - **DEFENSE OF OTHERS**
    - **Majority** — D stands in the shoes of person defended (that person must have had right to use force in self-defense)
    - **Minority** — D not liable if reasonably believes that person defended was privileged to use force
  - **DEFENSE OF PROPERTY**
    - Must make prior demand that D cease (or show that demand would be futile) before using force
    - May never use deadly force

ASSAULT

- **ACT** — must be volitional act
- **INTENT** — to cause someone to be apprehensive of receiving a harmful or offensive contact*
- **HARM** — resulting apprehension of an imminent harmful or offensive contact
- **DEFENSES** — all battery defenses

KAPLAN pmbr

1. INTENTIONAL TORTS: PERSONAL AND EMOTIONAL INJURY (*continued*)

FALSE IMPRISONMENT

ACT — must be volitional act

INTENT — to confine someone

RESULT — actual confinement of P; reasonable means of escape does *not* include —
- Having to leave property
- Dangerous means of escape
- Unreasonably embarrassing means of escape

HARM — knowledge of confinement *or* injury resulting from confinement

DEFENSES —
- All battery defenses
- Lawful arrest
- **Shopkeepers Privilege** — merchant may detain a suspected shoplifter for a reasonable time if he has probable cause that P is stealing and the shopkeeper does not use excessive force (Shopkeeper is still liable for actual injuries)

INTENTIONAL INFLICTION OF EMOTIONAL DISTRESS

ACT — extreme and outrageous conduct

INTENT — to cause severe emotional upset to P or recklessness with regard to P's upset

HARM — resulting emotional distress of a significant nature

DEFENSES —
- All battery defenses
- D's lack of knowledge of P's unusual susceptibility to emotional upset

NOTE: If D has the intent to commit (1) battery, (2) assault, (3) false imprisonment, (4) trespass to land, or (5) trespass to chattels and ends up causing an injury protected by any other of these five torts, the intent requirement is satisfied.

2. INTENTIONAL TORTS: INJURY TO PROPERTY

TRESPASS TO LAND

- **ACT** — must be volitional act
- **INTENT** — to do act which results in trespass*
- **HARM** — invasion of P's right to exclusive possession of her land; no damages need be proven, and once D has committed a trespass he is liable for all injuries to P's land, buildings, and chattels, even if unforeseeable
- **DEFENSES**
  - Consent of person in lawful possession
  - Entry to reclaim D's own property on P's land
  - Entry under public or private necessity
  - Entry to abate public or private nuisance

TRESPASS TO CHATTELS

- **ACT** — must be volitional act
- **INTENT** — to do act which results in trespass*
- **HARM** — intermeddling with P's possessory rights in personal property
  - Injury to chattel
  - Dispossession (loss of use)
- **REMEDY** — diminution of value (or cost of repair) and/or reasonable rental value
- **DEFENSES**
  - Consent
  - Necessity

CONVERSION

- **ACT** — must be volitional act
- **INTENT** — to exercise dominion and control over chattel which in fact belongs to P
- **HARM** — substantial interference with P's rights to use and enjoy his chattel
- **REMEDY** — P may require D to pay full market value of chattel
- **DEFENSES**
  - Consent
  - Necessity

NOTE: If D has the intent to commit (1) battery, (2) assault, (3) false imprisonment, (4) trespass to land, or (5) trespass to chattels and ends up causing an injury protected by any other of these five torts, the intent requirement is satisfied.

3. DEFAMATION

DEFAMATORY STATEMENT — one which subjects P to hatred, contempt, or ridicule (1st Restatement) or which lowers the esteem in which P is held by third parties (2nd Restatement)

OF OR CONCERNING P — someone must recognize that the statement is about this particular P

- P must be a living human being

Group defamation
- **Small group (less than 25)** — all members may have action even if statement is not all-inclusive
- **Medium group (between 25 and 150)** — may give each member a cause of action if all-inclusive
- **Large group (over 150)** — no member may sue even if statement is all-inclusive

PUBLICATION — at least one third party must hear the statement and understand its defamatory nature; D must be at least negligent with regard to the publication

PROOF OF SPECIAL DAMAGES OR EXCEPTION (a prima facie case requirement, *not* a rule of damages)

Special Damages — pecuniary loss resulting from a third party's response to the defamatory statement

Exceptions
- **Slander per se** — oral statements relating to: (1) incompetence in trade or profession, (2) present loathsome disease, (3) commission of serious crime, *or* (4) serious sexual misconduct
- **Libel (written statements)** — in some states all libel is actionable without proof of special damages, but common law required special damages unless libel is
  - **On its face** — (no innuendo or external knowledge is required to understand the statement's defamatory nature) *or*
  - **Per quod** — (innuendo or external knowledge is required to understand the statement's defamatory nature) *if* defamation relates to a slander per se category

DEFENSES

Truth must go to defamatory sting

Absolute Privileges (not defeated by even spite or knowledge of falsity) — (1) legislative proceeding, (2) judicial proceedings, (3) other official statements of governmental officials, (4) equal time broadcasts, and (5) communications between spouses

Common Law Qualified Privileges (defeated by spite or ill will, knowledge of falsity or reckless disregard of truth, and, perhaps, negligence) — (1) statements in D's own interest, (2) statements in the interest of third persons, (3) statements in the interest of the public, (4) reports of public proceedings, and (5) fair comment opinions

First Amendment Qualified Privileges
- **Public Officials, Candidates for Public Office, and Well-Known Public Figures** — must prove "malice" as defined by *NY Times v Sullivan* (that D knew statement was false or acted in reckless disregard of truth)
- **Limited Public Figures** — ordinary persons who *voluntarily* inject themselves into a public controversy are treated as public figures if alleged defamation relates to their position in the controversy but are treated as private persons if defamation concerns other matters
- **Private Persons** — must prove negligence with regard to truth when defendant is a member of the media; jurisdictions split when D is a private person

DAMAGES (once prima facie case, including existence of some special damages or exceptions, is made)

All special damages (defined above), including lost customers and lost employment
- Damage to P's reputation
- Damage to P's feelings, including medical bills attributable to P's emotional distress
- Punitive damages (when appropriate)

Note: When First Amendment qualified privilege applies, only actual damages (i.e., those proven with reasonable certainty by P) and not punitive damages may be recovered unless P proves malice

4. NEGLIGENCE

DUTY

Forseeable Plaintiff
- Cardozo — no duty owed to persons outside geographic zone of danger at the time of D's negligence
- Andrews — if D has breached a duty to anyone, duty is owed to everyone
- Rescuers are always foreseeable Ps

Omission
— as a general rule, there is not duty to act or aid another. The exceptions include:
- Duty to alleviate consequences of his own act endangers others (perhaps even if D's act was not even negligent)
- Duty to control others (e.g., children)
- Special relationship between P and D including:
  - contractual duty
  - innkeepers and guest
  - common carriers and passengers
  - school and pupils
- Undertaking to act — may not abandon an attempted rescue if D leaves P's in a worse condition

NOTE: Always consider cause-in-fact issue in all omission problems

4. NEGLIGENCE *(continued)*

STANDARDS OF CARE

Reasonable Person Standard — what would a reasonable person have done in those circumstances. Balance (1) likelihood of harm and (2) gravity of potential injury against (3) social utility of D's actual conduct and (4) burden of adequate precautions. *Always state what D should have done.*

- Mental characteristics of adult defendant irrelevant
- Physical characteristics of adult defendant may be considered
- Children must act as would children of the same age, experience, and intelligence except that they are measured by adult standards when they are engaged in adult activities
- Emergency situation will lower D's standard if, but only if, D's own negligence did not cause emergency
- Community custom is relevant to establishing what is reasonable, but it is not determinative

Standards for Professionals (Malpractice) — the minimum common skill of members in good standing in the profession. Expert testimony is required except when negligence is obvious

- **Locality Rule** — at common law, conduct of general practitioners was measured by what others in the same or similar localities would do (today, locality rule is simply a factor in most states)
- **Specialists** — held to national standard

Statutes — if statute establishes *civil* liability, it conclusively establishes standard. If criminal statute ask (1) is P in a class that the statute was designed to protect (2) was he to be protected from this type of harm; if answer to both questions is "yes" then

- **Negligence Per Se (majority rule)** — D may not introduce evidence as to reasonableness, although she may argue for an implied exception (i.e., because of the unique circumstances of this case, what she did was inherently more reasonable than what the statute required)
- **Presumption of Negligence** — D may argue that his conduct was nevertheless reasonable despite the statute, but has the burden of proving this
- **Evidence of Negligence** — violation merely helps P establish his prima facie case (Note: Most jurisdictions follow this rule for violation of local ordinances.)
- **Caveat** — under any of these views the issues of cause-in-fact, proximate cause, and compensible damage issues are the same as in any other negligence action. Contributory negligence and assumption of risk issues are also the same except when statute was designed to protect P from his own folly

Special Standards

- **Automotive Guests** — under "guest statutes" existing in many states, an automobile driver is liable to a non-paying guest only if the driver was reckless
- **Owners and Occupiers of Land**
- **Innkeepers and Common Carriers** — owe "highest" duty of care

BREACH

Normally, simply a question of fact

- **Res Ipsa Loquitur** — circumstantial evidence of negligence arises when
  - Accident is one that normally does not occur in the absence of negligence
  - Instrumentality causing injury is under D's exclusive control or D is responsible for all others in control
  - P must introduce evidence removing any inference of his own fault

Concurrent Conduct — even conduct which is not negligent by itself will be actionable if it combines with similar conduct of others if the other's conduct was foreseeable

(continued)

4. NEGLIGENCE *(continued)*

CAUSE-IN-FACT (Actual Cause)

- **"But for" Test** — normally, ask if injury would have occurred but for that aspect of D's conduct which was negligent
- **Substantial Factor Test** — when two or more causes concur to cause an event but either alone would have been sufficient to cause injury, each is a cause-in-fact if it is a substantial factor in causing the injury
- When two or more Ds are negligent but P cannot prove whose negligence caused the injury, court may shift burden of disproving causation to Ds
- Look for cause-in-fact issues in all omission problems

PROXIMATE CAUSE (Legal Cause)

- **Spotting the Issue — look for**
  - Minor negligence causing tremendous injury
  - Freakish results
  - Multiple persons or factors contributing to the injury

- **Basic Rules**
  - **Direct Injury Cases (i.e., there are no intervening causes between D's negligence and P's injury)**
    - Injury to Persons — all direct causes are proximate
    - Injury to Property
      - Traditional View — all direct causes are proximate
      - Trend — was this injury a foreseeable result of D's conduct?
  - **Indirect Injury Cases — was this injury a foreseeable result of D's conduct (even if the exact way in which the injury occurred was unforeseeable)?**

- **Decided Cases**
  - Subsequent negligence, including medical malpractice, is always foreseeable
  - Subsequent criminal acts or intentional tortious conduct are not normally foreseeable, but may be foreseeable if that risk is what made D's conduct negligent in the first place
  - An attempted rescue is always foreseeable
  - Acts of nature are generally unforeseeable
  - Suicide is unforeseeable unless it was the result of an uncontrollable impulse caused by D's negligence

DAMAGES

- **Emotional Injury — recoverable only if there is some accompanying physical injury**
  - Only a few states (including Florida) still require impact
  - Trend is to allow recovery even if emotional injury was not caused by P's concern for her own safety
- **Pure economic injury not protectible by negligence cause of action**

5. DEFENSES TO NEGLIGENCE

Normally, the issue of P's contributory negligence is controlled by the same rules as those governing D's negligence, except that the mental defects of an adult P may be considered

Imputed Contributory Negligence — as a general rule, the negligence of a third party will be imputed to P only if P would have been vicariously liable for the third party's negligence if P had been the defendant

CONTRIBUTORY NEGLIGENCE

Effect of a finding of contributory negligence

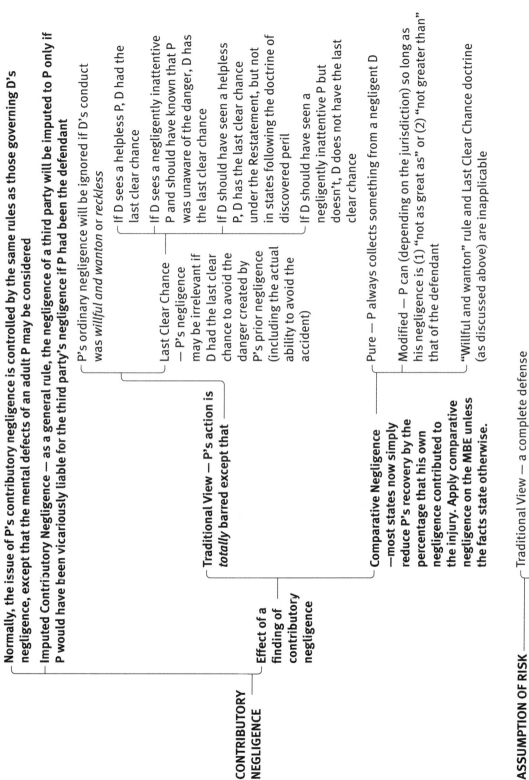

P's ordinary negligence will be ignored if D's conduct was *willful and wanton or reckless*

    If D sees a helpless P, D had the last clear chance

    If D sees a negligently inattentive P and should have known that P was unaware of the danger, D has the last clear chance

Last Clear Chance — P's negligence may be irrelevant if D had the last clear chance to avoid the danger created by P's prior negligence (including the actual ability to avoid the accident)

    If D should have seen a helpless P, D has the last clear chance under the Restatement, but not in states following the doctrine of discovered peril

    If D should have seen a negligently inattentive P but doesn't, D does not have the last clear chance

Traditional View — P's action is *totally* barred except that

Pure — P always collects something from a negligent D

Modified — P can (depending on the jurisdiction) so long as his negligence is (1) "not as great as" or (2) "not greater than" that of the defendant

"Willful and wanton" rule and Last Clear Chance doctrine (as discussed above) are inapplicable

Comparative Negligence —most states now simply reduce P's recovery by the percentage that his own negligence contributed to the injury. Apply comparative negligence on the MBE unless the facts state otherwise.

ASSUMPTION OF RISK — when P actually understands the risk to his safety and voluntarily subjects himself to it

Traditional View — a complete defense

Comparative Negligence Jurisdictions — assumption of risk is normally treated as an aspect of contributory negligence (and is thus only a partial bar), but may still be a total bar when D's only duty was to warn (as in certain landowner and products liability cases)

6. PRODUCTS LIABILITY

MISREPRESENTATION
Under Restatement 402(B)

Gravamen — public misrepresentation of material fact

Possible Defendants — any commercial seller

Possible Plaintiffs — anyone relying on the representation

Defenses
- Assumption of risk
- Misuse of product

EXPRESS WARRANTY
Under UCC 2-313

Gravamen — breach of express warranty

Possible Defendants — any seller (liability to remote purchasers governed by UCC 2-318 [discussed below])

Possible Plaintiffs (UCC 2-318)
- **Alternative A (majority)** — buyer, members of his household, and guests in his home
  (but privity requirement may be eased by caselaw)
- **Alternatives B and C** — anyone expected to use, consumer, or be affected by the goods

NOTE: liability under Alternative A and B is limited to personal injuries

Defenses
- Assumption of risk
- Misuse of Product
- Failure to give prompt notice of breach to D
- "Disclaimer" can explain, but cannot cancel express warranty

NEGLIGENCE

Gravamen — breach of duty of care (same elements as ordinary negligence, but warning of danger may be sufficient)

Possible Defendants
- **Manufacturers** — liable for design defects and own negligence in handling
- **Retailers and Wholesalers**
  - liable for own negligence in handling
  - liable for negligence of predecessor when there is a duty to inspect as when
    - Product comes in damaged container
    - Prior problems with other products
    - Manufacturer of dubious reputation

Possible Plaintiffs — anyone foreseeably endangered

Defenses
- Contributory negligence
- Assumption of risk

6. PRODUCTS LIABILITY *(continued)*

STRICT PRODUCTS LIABILITY
(or Absolute Liability in Tort)
under Restatement 402(A)

Gravamen ⎯
- Defective product
- Defect must make product unreasonably dangerous for use or consumption

Possible Defendants — anyone engaged in commercial distribution

Possible Plaintiffs — anyone endangered by defect

Defenses ⎯
- Assumption of risk
- Misuse of product

IMPLIED WARRANTY
under UCC 2-314 to 2-318

Breach of Implied Warranty of ⎯
- Merchantability — goods must be of fair average quality and fit for ordinary purpose
- Fitness for Particular Purpose — goods must be fit for special use if buyer relied on seller's judgement in recommending the product

Possible Defendants ⎯
- Merchantability — merchants in goods of that kind
- Fitness for Particular Purpose — any seller with special knowledge

Possible Plaintiffs (UCC 2-318) — same as express warranty (above)

Liability to remote purchasers governed by UCC 2-318

Defenses — same as express warranty (above)

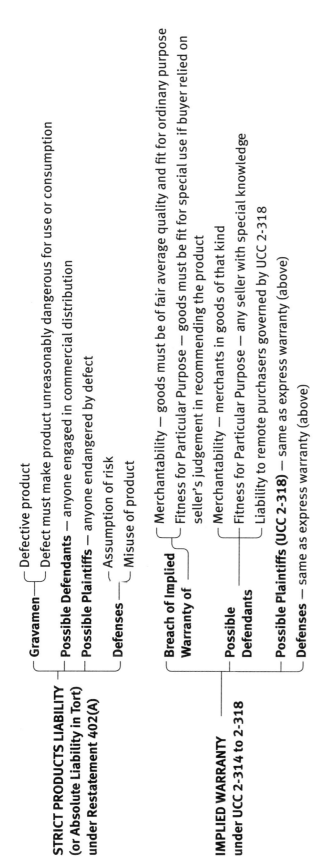

NOTES

KAPLAN) *pmbr*

NOTES

KAPLAN) prehr

NOTES

KAPLAN) *pmbr*

NOTES